CHARLESTON
The Delaplaine
2020 *Long Weekend Guide*

NO BUSINESS HAS PAID A SINGLE PENNY OR GIVEN *ANYTHING* TO BE INCLUDED IN THIS BOOK.

Andrew Delaplaine

A list of the author's other travel guides, as well as his political thrillers, can be found at the end of this book.

Senior Editors
Renee & Sophie Delaplaine

Gramercy Park Press
New York – Paris – London

Copyright © by Gramercy Park Press
All rights reserved.

Please submit corrections, additions or comments to
andrewdelaplaine@mac.com

CHARLESTON
The Delaplaine Long Weekend Guide

TABLE OF CONTENTS

Chapter 1 – WHY CHARLESTON? – 4

Chapter 2 – GETTING ABOUT – 7

Chapter 3 – WHERE TO STAY – 9
High on the Hog / Sensible Alternatives / On a Budget

Chapter 4 – WHERE TO EAT - 20
Ridiculously Extravagant
Sensible Alternatives
Quality Bargain Spots

Chapter 5 – NIGHTLIFE – 77

Chapter 6 – WHAT TO SEE & DO – 81

Chapter 7 – SHOPPING & SERVICES -106

INDEX – 115

OTHER BOOKS BY THE SAME AUTHOR – 120

Chapter 1
WHY CHARLESTON?

The historic part of downtown is on a peninsula formed by two rivers, the Ashley and the Cooper, flowing into the Atlantic. It's got much the same geographical layout as Manhattan does, where you have the East and the Hudson Rivers merging at the tip of Manhattan.

But that's the only thing that will remind you of New York. Charleston was captured in the Civil War without much property damage, so the historic part of town has buildings that are hundreds of years old.

Most of the damage they suffered has come from hurricanes, not cannon balls. The current downtown skyline, with practically no tall buildings due to the city's height restriction ordinance, is dominated by church steeples and the stunning Arthur Ravenel cable-stay bridge completed in 2005 over the Cooper River. The city is a major port on the eastern seaboard of the U.S. and a popular destination for domestic and international tourists.

Charles Towne, as it was first called, was established in 1670 by Anthony Ashley Cooper on the west bank of the Ashley River, Charles Towne Landing, a few miles northwest of the present downtown. By 1680, the settlement had grown and moved to its current location on the peninsula.

Around 1690, the English colonists erected a fortification wall around the small settlement to aid in its defense. The wall sheltered the area, in the present French Quarter, from Cumberland Street south to Water Street, from Meeting Street east to East Bay Street. The wall was destroyed around 1720. Cobblestone lanes and one building remain from this Colonial English Walled Town: the **Powder Magazine**, where the town's supply of gunpowder was stored. Remnants of the Colonial wall were found beneath the **Old Exchange Building**.

Charleston was the first city in the U.S. to pass a historical preservation ordinance. Thus, much of the beautiful architecture, from early Colonial, Georgian, Federal, Greek Revival, and Italianate to Victorian, remains for future generations to see and enjoy.

Charleston is also known as the Holy City due to the numerous church steeples poking out of the low-rise skyline. Another reason: it was one of the few places in the original 13 colonies to provide religious tolerance to the French Huguenots as well as to Jews.

Chapter 2
GETTING ABOUT

BY FOOT
Once you're in the historic district, you won't need a car. If the walking is too much for you, hop board the DASH shuttles to move between sights on your list. You'll see the signs, but if you want more information, go to www.ridecarta.com

CHARLESTON BLACK CAB COMPANY
843-216-2627
www.charlestonblackcabcompany.com

They have roomy London-style taxis from the airport to downtown. If you're going to hire a car and driver while here, get one of these. Much more comfortable than regular cars. Use them to go to the plantations outside town.

GRAY TOURS
See listing under What To See & Do.

TOURS
There are many walking tours, which give you the opportunity to see more than just driving past in a bus or carriage. There is a walking tour for virtually every interest. You will find Pub Tours, Civil War tours, culinary tours, ghost tours, Gulla tours, architecture tours, art tours, and even pirate tours. Some of the walking tour companies offer tours with guides in period costume. Charleston Pirate Tours even has a costumed guide whose parrot, a blue and gold macaw, accompanies the tour.

BROAD STREET
In the historic district, there is a major east-west street, Broad Street, which divides two areas in historic downtown, aptly named *North of Broad* and *South of Broad*. Those South of Broad were nicknamed SOBs, and those Slightly North of Broad were SNOBs. The *French Quarter*, founded by the French Huguenots, is just south of the Market Area along the waterfront. The area near the southern tip of the peninsula, where the Ashley and Cooper Rivers meet, is known as *The Battery*.

Chapter 3
WHERE TO STAY

BATTERY CARRIAGE HOUSE INN
20 S Battery St, Charleston, 843-727-3100
www.batterycarriagehouse.com
Has 10 rooms a stone's throw from **White Point Gardens** at the Battery. I've stayed here several times and loved it every minute. Breakfast in a walled garden with shade trees in good weather.

BELMOND CHARLESTON PLACE HOTEL
Shops At Charleston Place
205 Meeting St, Charleston, 843-722-4900

www.belmond.com
Located in the city's historic district, this big old luxury hotel offers comfortable guestrooms (over 400 of them) decorated with classic Charleston-inspired furnishings. (There's also a concierge floor.) It's a bit musty, but you can't beat the location. Amenities include: marble bathrooms, minibar, cable TV, and free Wi-Fi. The hotel also features a spa, a gym, and a rooftop heated pool. On-site eateries – **Palmetto Café** and the **Charleston Grill** – are available, and they're both very good. The Grill features live jazz. The **Spa at Charleston Place** offers pampering spa services. Other amenities include: swimming pool, health club and business center.

CHARLESTON HARBOR RESORT & MARINA
20 Patriots Point Rd, Mt Pleasant, 888-856-0028
www.charlestonharborresort.com
Right across the Ravenel Bridge, this resort and marina on the harbor features 125 comfortable nautical-themed guestrooms. They operate a free trolley that will take you downtown. Amenities include: free Wi-Fi, HD TVs, iPod docks, and coffeemakers. Balconies, whirlpool tubs, and fireplaces are featured in some rooms. The resort includes a private beach, a seasonal outdoor pool, hot tub, gym, rooftop bar with live music, a poolside tiki bar and two restaurants.

THE DEWBERRY
334 Meeting St, Charleston, 843-558-8000
www.thedewberrycharleston.com
NEIGHBORHOOD: Mazyck-Wraggborough

Recently renovated and repurposed mid-century modern Federal building overlooking historic Marion Square, this thoroughly delightful hotel offers 155 rooms and suites furnished in an eclectic style. Charleston is not noted for its luxury hotels. Rather, the opposite. At the bar here you'll find servers in crips white jackets stirring cocktails the old-fashioned way. Amenities: Complimentary Wi-Fi, flat-screen TVs, minibars and premium bedding. Hotel features: full-service spa, on-sight restaurant, **Henrietta's Brasserie,** featuring Southern cuisine and a raw bar with novel items like pickled shrimp and crab Louie. There's also a fitness center, and massage/treatment rooms. Conveniently located near the Charleston Museum and the South Carolina Aquarium.

FRANCIS MARION HOTEL
387 King St, Charleston, 843-722-0600
www.francismarionhotel.com/
Located opposite Marion Square, this famous hotel offers 235 rooms – including 10 suites and 7 penthouse suites. It's not as much fun to stay in as one of the nicer B&Bs, but if you like big hotels, this will do. Amenities include: free Wi-Fi, fitness center, non-smoking rooms, and flat-panel TVs. On site conveniences include The **Swamp Fox Restaurant and Bar**, Spa Adagio Day Spa, Starbucks Coffee Shop, and Gift Shop. No pets allowed.

FRENCH QUARTER INN
166 Church St, Charleston, 843-722-1900
www.fqicharleston.com

Located in downtown Charleston, this 50-room inn offers comfortable guestrooms. Known for its expert service and smart staff. You'll get a glass of champagne when you check in, and in the evening, they serve wine and canapés like smoked salmon. Before you turn in, they'll serve you a glass of port (or milk & cookies for you teetotalers out there). Very English, right? Amenities include: flat screen TVs, Blu-Ray DVD players, and Wi-Fi access. On-site spa and massage services available.

HAMPTON INN-HISTORIC DISTRICT
345 Meeting St, Charleston, 843-723-4000
www.hamptoninn3.hilton.com
 Is in a restored warehouse just old enough to be billed as the area's only antebellum hotel, with a fitness center, pool and 170 rooms.

THE HOLIDAY INN HOTEL CHARLESTON HISTORIC DISTRICT
425 Meeting St, Charleston, 843-718-2327
www.ihg.com
 Near Marion Square Park and shop-filled King Street. The concierge can be a big help to you.

JOHN RUTLEDGE HOUSE INN
116 Broad St, Charleston, 843-723-7999
www.johnrutledgehouseinn.com
This inn, a National Historic Landmark, is a great example of Charleston's history. The Inn features 19 elegant guestrooms and suites set in the main house or two carriage houses, guests are treated with the personalized service of a bed and breakfast. Nice views over Broad Street as you enjoy coffee on the second-floor piazza. Breakfast is served in the parlor of this 250-year-old house. Amenities include: free breakfast and afternoon tea, flat screen TVs, DVD player, free bottled water, and free wireless internet.

KINGS COURTYARD INN
198 King St, Charleston, 800-845-6119
www.kingscourtyardinn.com
Located in the center of the historic district, this inn features beautifully restored rooms fitting for this 1853 historic mansion. Amenities include: hard wood floors, working fireplaces in some rooms, free breakfast, evening wine & cheese reception, and free wireless internet.

THE MARKET PAVILION HOTEL
225 E Bay St, Charleston, 843-723-0500
www.marketpavilion.com
High-end extravagance. 60 luxurious rooms with mahogany furniture and four-poster beds and other antiques. Rooftop bars are popular in Charleston because the town is on a peninsula, sweeping views are commonplace. You can't do better than the rooftop bar here, near City Market. A great view of

the harbor. There's plexiglass around the edges and heaters are brought out in cold weather so it's still a good bet. **Grille 225** is street level in this hotel.

MIDDLETON PLACE
4290 Ashley River Rd, Charleston, 843-556-0500
www.theinnatmiddletonplace.com
Beautiful unique accommodations in a historic inn with 55 rooms just a short walk from the historic landmark Middleton Place. Variety of luxury amenities and features including a swimming pool, hiking, kayaking and horseback riding. Beautiful plantation with centuries-old gardens. Complimentary breakfast.

MILLS HOUSE
115 Meeting St, Charleston, 843-577-2400
www.millshouse.com
This charming hotel first opened in 1853 and is now a full service hotel with complete hospitality staff. Luxury accommodations offer beautiful views of the historic district. Amenities include: free Wi-Fi, LCD TV with pay per view channels, outdoor pool and fitness center. On-site restaurant, lounge, and gift shop. Conveniently located downtown near historic attractions and shopping.

NOTSO-HOSTEL
156 Spring St, Charleston, 843-722-8383
www.notsohostel.com
This unique hostel offers simple, clean lodgings. Conveniently located near shops, restaurants, bars, and museums. Amenities include: free breakfast and

Wi-Fi. Free parking. Lodgings vary among dorms, private rooms and camping. Kitchens and bathrooms are communal. Hammocks and ping pong tables in the backyard.

PLANTERS INN
112 N Market St, Charleston, 843-722-2345
www.plantersinn.com
Located in the heart of the historic district, this award-winning 64-room inn offers comfortable understated elegantly plush lodgings. They're tried to replicate what a private home would be like with nice touches like Oriental rugs, lots of antiques and 4-posters. Excellent staff. Amenities include: free Wi-Fi, babysitting/childcare, free newspapers in lobby, and on-site bar.

TWO MEETING STREET INN
2 Meeting St, Charleston, 843-723-7322
www.twomeetingstreetinn.com
This romantic historic bed and breakfast on Battery Park offers luxury lodgings with only 9 elegant guestrooms. This is the oldest inn in Charleston. the rooms are stuffed with antiques like tiffany stained-glass windows, Venetian glass fixtures, Audubon prints decorating the walls. At sundown, relax in a rocking chair on the porch and look out over the harbor. Amenities include: free Southern breakfast, daily newspapers, Lowcountry afternoon tea, evening sherry, and free Wi-Fi.

WENTWORTH MANSION
149 Wentworth St, Charleston, 843-853-1886
www.wentworthmansion.com
This beautifully restored four-story brick historic mansion (built by a cotton baron in 1886 with red Philadelphia bricks) offers 21 elegant rooms with marble fireplaces and Tiffany stained glass, oversized soaking tubs. Modern items like flat-screen TVs are here, but you'll love the crystal chandeliers and the marble mantelpieces. This hotel has luxurious amenities and is conveniently located near dining, art, history, and shopping. Free breakfast and nightly homemade chocolates. Excellent dining on-site at the **Circa 1996** restaurant. On-site spa and athletic club in what were formerly the stables. There's even an area in the garden for pets. Oh, be sure to check out

the cupola atop the hotel—it has superlative views of the city.

ZERO GEORGE
0 George St, Charleston, 843-817-7900
www.zerogeorge.com
Set in a private landscaped courtyard enclave, these lodgings at the base of George Street are a collection of 5 restored 19th Century historic townhouses surrounding a courtyard paved with oyster shells and stones. There's a mix of Old South tradition that has been successfully combined with contemporary décor and furnishings. There are 18 simple and elegant guest rooms. You'll like sitting on the verandah having a drink as you look out over the lush landscaping, or get lost in the little pocket gardens. The carriage house dating from 1804 is where they serve breakfast. Located in the upscale **Ansonborough** neighborhood, Zero George is close to narrow little pre-Revolutionary War streets with

cobblestones and lots of restaurants, bars, cafes and shops, ranging from Gucci to a store that sells local honey. While it's close to lots of the top eateries in town, it has its own café that's not too shabby either: get the organic chicken tacos and tempura green beans. Excellent choice.

Chapter 4
WHERE TO EAT

The culinary world was upended when for three years running, a restaurant from Charleston took high honors when it snagged the prestigious James Beard Award for Best Southeastern Chef (**Hominy Grill** took the honors first, followed by **Fig**, then **McCrady's**). Things have never been the same since.

    That being said, the one meal you must have to get the feeling of old Charleston is a Lowcountry Oyster Roast. They do them all year-round at **<u>Bowens Island</u>** (see listing below). You eat roasted oysters and huge hushpuppies and you'll never be happier. Bowens is on stilts over the marsh. The oysters (they call them "cluster oysters") come directly from the water and are steamed open on metal sheets over a brick-lined pit. A wood fire is important because the smoke is essential to create the unforgettable taste. All you need is lemon to finish them off when they are laid out before you. (Some like Tabasco.) Beer is the drink of choice.

Let's talk Fried Chicken, shall we? You'll see it on every menu. In "The Virginia House-Wife" by Mary Randolph, published in 1824, you'll find the first recipe for Southern Fried Chicken: "Cut [the chicken] up as for the fricassee, dredge the pieces well with flour, sprinkle them with salt, put them into a good quantity of boiling lard, and fry them a light brown."

Can't get much simpler than that. And yet such simplicity has allowed the term "fried chicken" to be interpreted in hundreds of thousands of different ways, almost all of them perfectly wonderful, to my mind, having been raised in South Carolina on a plantation. With slaves adding spices redolent of their West African homeland, the variations on the theme exploded, and continue to unfold today. Even in the finest of fine restaurants, you'll find world-renowned chefs unable to shake the urge to put their signature touch to this most American of all-American foods.

167 RAW
289 E Bay St, Charleston, 843-579-4997
www.167raw.com
CUISINE: Seafood/Seafood Market
DRINKS: Beer & Wine Only
SERVING: Lunch & Dinner; closed Sun
PRICE RANGE: $$
NEIGHBORHOOD: Ansonborough

Casual seafood eatery popular with locals and tourists. It's got an ultra-casual atmosphere, with menu items scribbled on a mirror. Framed fishing guides hang on the white-tiled walls. Seafood selections include oysters, lobster rolls, fish tacos, shrimp tacos, and ceviche. Favorites: Tuna Burger and Lobster roll. Nice wine list. Usually a line, so be prepared to wait.

BERTHA'S KITCHEN
2332 Meeting St Rd, North Charleston, 843-554-6519
http://runinout.com/Bertha
CUISINE: Southern; soul food
DRINKS: No Booze
SERVING: Lunch & Dinner
PRICE RANGE: $
Up on the less fashionable northern end of Meeting Street you'll find Bertha's. Perfectly executed soul food. Fried pork chops, lima beans, mac-n-cheese, okra soup, collard greens, yams, baked chicken (a

dish often ignored by tourists who don't know how good it can be), stew beef.

BOWENS ISLAND RESTAURANT
1870 Bowens Island Rd, Charleston, 843-795-2757
www.bowensisland.biz
CUISINE: Seafood; oyster roast
DRINKS: Full Bar
SERVING: Dinner; closed Sun & Mon
PRICE RANGE: $$$
A local seafood institution that offers counter service, a bar, waterfront views, and authentic seafood dishes.

Favorites include: Fresh oysters, Fried Chicken Breast strips and Crab cakes. This no-frills two-level eatery is a favorite of locals and tourists. Customers had scrawled graffiti on every inch of its walls. But when it reopened atop 18-foot stilts, it boasted a much better view and a superior screened in deck overlooking Folly Creek. Spend time reading all the new graffiti (or add some of your own) while you wait for the roasted oysters. Always crowded. Always worth it.

BUTCHER & BEE
1085 Morrison Dr, Charleston, 843-619-0202
www.butcherandbee.com
CUISINE: Sandwiches
DRINKS: No Booze; BYOB
SERVING: Lunch & Dinner
PRICE RANGE: $$
Popular eatery known for their fresh creative sandwiches. (They even make the bread for the famous **McCrady's**.) Great place for a casual brunch. The French toast is tasty and they make a delicious baked egg and tomato with tahini. There's an herb garden out back. Each sandwich is like a work of art. It's open late and attracts a lot of chefs after their own restaurants have closed for the night. BYOB.

CANNON GREEN
103 Spring St, Charleston, 843-817-6299
www.cannongreencharleston.com
CUISINE: Mediterranean
DRINKS: Full Bar

SERVING: Dinner Tues- Sat; Lunch on Sun; Closed on Mon
PRICE RANGE: $$$
NEIGHBORHOOD: Cannonborough
Executive Chef Amalia Scatena (who trained in Italy) offers an a la carte menu of seasonal Mediterranean fare. Menu picks: Cioppino (the best in the whole state, I'm sure), Raviolo and Shrimp & Grits. Elegant eatery, popular choice for weddings, the restaurant serves innovative cocktails and has an impressive wine list. Great choice for Sunday Brunch. Reservations recommended.

CAVIAR AND BANANAS
College of Charleston
51 George St, Charleston, 843-577-7757
www.caviarandbananas.com
CUISINE: Breakfast/Sandwiches
DRINKS: Beer & Wine Only
SERVING: Breakfast, Lunch & Dinner (closes at 8 p.m.)
PRICE RANGE: $$
A combination gourmet market and café offering a bountiful menu of sandwiches, salads, sushi, and treats like their Duck Confit Panini. Great spot for breakfast or to collect items for a picnic.

CHARLESTON GRILL
224 King St, Charleston, 843-577-4522
www.charlestongrill.com
CUISINE: American
DRINKS: Full Bar
SERVING: Dinner
PRICE RANGE: $$$$

A grand ballroom of a restaurant tucked away in a posh hotel. From a glamorous banquette, you can take in the sophisticated tunes of the Quentin Baxter Ensemble and the very polite antics of practically all of Charleston, from dads and debutantes to Gullah painters. Snack on the truffle parmesan popcorn and a kiwi version of the Pimm's Cup. General Manager Mickey Bakst and his staff have carefully created an ambiance that is all at once mellow and lively, traditional and contemporary. Soft jazz bounces off of wood-paneled walls and crisp, white tablecloths. Servers trained in the French tradition delight guests with each menu suggestion and wine pairing. Seamless service, orchestrated by the attentive, knowledgeable and approachable staff, sets the stage for an unforgettable dining experience.

CHEZ NOUS
6 Payne Ct, Charleston, 843-579-3060
www.cheznouschs.com
CUISINE: French
DRINKS: Beer & Wine Only
SERVING: Lunch & Dinner; closed Mon.
PRICE RANGE: $$$
NEIGHBORHOOD: Cannonborough
Small neighborhood eatery with a daily-changing international menu with just two appetizers, 2 entrees and 2 desserts. Payne Street is not a touristy area, and the restaurant is housed in a classic two-story house, so you'll feel like you're eating in someone's home. Nice selection of French wines.

CHUBBY FISH
252 Coming St, 854-222-3949
www.chubbyfishcharleston.com
CUISINE: Seafood/Tapas
DRINKS: Full Bar
SERVING: Dinner, Closed Sun & Mon.
PRICE RANGE: $$$
NEIGHBORHOOD: Downtown / Cannonborough
Ultra-simple small neighborhood eatery featuring creative seafood-focused menu all written out for you on a blackboard (that's raised above the open kitchen) listing raw bar items, whole fish available that day, small plates and large plates. Oysters from the

Carolinas and other Southern states are featured. Favorites: Smoked Bluefish with curry rice; roasted bone marrow with crispy rock shrimp; Grouper Cheeks with chive butter; Chicken-fried swordfish collar. For a treat try the tempura-battered frog legs. But beware that the menu changes with whatever's fresh, fresh, fresh. That said, you can't go wrong here. Impressive wine list and wine pairings for such a tiny establishment.

CIRCA 1886
149 Wentworth St., 843-853-7828
www.circa1886.com
CUISINE: American
DRINKS: Full bar

SERVING: Mon - Sat, dinner from 5:30, closed Sun; a little dressy; no shorts, etc.
PRICE RANGE: $$$$

Chef Marc Collins is the star here, and he allows influences from around the world to help him forge the unusual Lowcountry food he serves here. Think less butter and less fat. Think whole grains. Menu is decidedly and intentional very seasonal in keeping with the craze that has engulfed Charleston in recent years. Grilled quail with a spicy plum sauce and smoked cheddar grits; hearts of palm in a passion fruit vinaigrette; pork shoulder with "coffee essence," mustard greens and a sour orange hollandaise; lamb served with sweet potato celery root and cauliflower gremolata; wild mushroom pot pie. Don't ignore Pastry Chef Lovorn's delicacies: peaches & cream soufflé, strawberry shortcake (we were there in August when the fruit was perfect). This place is so good it makes you want to move here permanently.

COAST
39 D John St, Charleston, 843-722-8838
www.coastbarandgrill.com
CUISINE: Seafood, Cajun & Creole
DRINKS: Full Bar
SERVING: Dinner
PRICE RANGE: $$

A casual, hip restaurant in a former indigo warehouse. (Quick—do you know what indigo is?) It has open oak grills and tin-roofed booths that draw savvy locals. The menu, which specializes in local seafood, has a Creole twist.

THE CODFATHER, PROPER FISH & CHIPS
4254 Spruill Ave, 843-789-4649
No Website
CUISINE: Fish & Chips, Seafood
DRINKS: Beer & Wine
SERVING: Lunch & Dinner, Closed Sun & Mon.
PRICE RANGE: $$
NEIGHBORHOOD: North Charleston
Known as the only place in town to get proper fish and chips made the traditional British way. Fish is always nice and crisp, malt vinegar, the works. (They even serve those mushy peas you get in England, only they're better here.) Also, fresh baked British style meat pies and sausage rolls. Nice selection of draft beer from the old country. Bare bones interior with a mural on the wall that tries its damnedest to provide a little "atmosphere," but it's the fish & chips you want. A few picnic tables under umbrellas outside, if you like.

DARLING OYSTER BAR
513 King St, 843-641-0821
www.thedarling.com
CUISINE: Seafood/Raw Bar
DRINKS: Full Bar
SERVING: Dinner, Late night
PRICE RANGE: $$
NEIGHBORHOOD: Radcliffeborough
Trendy eatery in a century-old building with high ceilings, tall windows looking out into the street, a busy vibe, white-tiled floors and a beautiful long bar where you can get counter service for the Darling's creative seafood-focused menu or just have drinks.

Tables along the side and in the back provide a lower-key, more private experience. Super place I really loved. Favorites: Raw oysters; Baked oysters with bacon; Shrimp & Grits with Cheddar, country ham and fennel; Fried fish baskets. Get a side order of the hush puppies with sorghum butter. Daily seafood specials. Oyster shooters are a must—just to get you started.

DAVE's CARRY-OUT
42 Morris St., Charleston, 843-577-7943
No Website
CUISINE: Seafood; soul food
DRINKS: Full Bar
SERVING: Lunch (11-3), dinner (5-11); closed Sunday
PRICE RANGE: $

I always find it amusing that people will go to **McCrady's** and **Husk** and pay a New York dollar for what is really just tarted up Southern cuisine you can get at lots of places without all the fuss and white tablecloths. No one fries shrimp this—what's the word?—*lightly.* It's just enough batter and then it's like they flash fry the shrimp. Whole fried flounder, fish sandwich, all the side dishes are good. Pure excellence. (Call ahead before you make a special trip—they sometimes close without any notice. They just lock the door and leave. Maybe they go shrimping. Whenever I ask, they just shrug.)

EARLY BIRD DINER
1644 Savannah Hwy, Charleston, 843-277-2353
www.earlybirddiner.com
CUISINE: American
DRINKS: No Booze
SERVING: Breakfast, Lunch & Dinner
PRICE RANGE: $
A funky diner inspired eatery filled with art with a menu of American diner classics. The excellent coffee comes from a local roaster, King Bean. Staff here are blunt, no frills, to the point. A big locals' hangout. Menu favorites include: Fried chicken with mushroom gravy and Fettuccine with vegetables. Great selection of desserts that changes daily.

EDMUND'S OAST
1081 Morrison Dr, Charleston. 843-727-1145
www.edmundsoast.com
CUISINE: Gastropub
DRINKS: Full Bar
SERVING: Dinner nightly
PRICE RANGE: $$
Find out why this spot was included on the 100 Best Southern Restaurants list. A hip e`atery with a

creative menu of American favorites. Great brunch destination. Bar features four dozen beers on tap including several house beers. The beers go just fine with their homemade pickled shrimp. Menu favorites include: Lamb meatballs, heritage pumpkin custard, chicken & rice porridge and Chocolate Mousse with caramel.

EVO PIZZERIA & CRAFT BAKERY
1075 E Montague Ave, 843-225-1796
www.evopizza.com
CUISINE: Pizza
DRINKS: Beer & Wine
SERVING: Lunch & Dinner
PRICE RANGE: $$$
NEIGHBORHOOD: North Charleston / Park Circle
Casual eatery in a nondescript red-brick building doesn't do justice to the quality of food served in this place offering wood-fired pizza with recipes that change during the seasons, a nice touch, so you might get a pizza with pumpkin on it during Halloween. Everything is fresh from the mozzarella to the pizza dough. Everything is fresh. Can I say that a third time? Besides offering some 10 pizza selections (Pastrami & Corn; Chorizo & Tomato; Pork Trifecta, for example), they also have great sandwiches, good salads, and starters like Wood-fired olives (so flavorful). Impressive list of beers and ciders. Next door they have a **Craft Bakery** with excellent out-of-this-world sandwiches and dinner specials. I'm getting used to the red brick.

FIG
232 Meeting St, Charleston, 843-805-5900
www.eatatfig.com
CUISINE: American
DRINKS: Full Bar
SERVING: Dinner
PRICE RANGE: $$$

I mentioned earlier that the chef here, **Mike Lata**, is a James Beard Award winner, so you can expect only the finest ingredients prepared (and served) expertly. The menu always has new items on it, but one thing that's always on the menu—the fish stew en cocotte (cooked in ramekins). This is a flavorful stew with a strong scent of saffron in the broth that's simply divine. In it you'll find white shrimp, squid, mussels, fingerling potatoes, rouille. Other selections might include Rebellion Farms suckling pig, clams steamed in capers, flounder dusted in corn flour. The side dishes (order for the table) might be beets, fresh greens, farrotto. Mike usually lists the farms where the food originated, even down to the lettuces. FIG, by the way, stands for "Food Is Good." (Because the food everywhere is *not* always good, I would change that to "Fig Is Good.")

FOLLY BEACH CRAB SHACK
26 Center St, Folly Beach, 843-588-3080
www.crabshacks.com
CUISINE: Seafood/American
DRINKS: Full Bar
SERVING: Lunch & Dinner
PRICE RANGE: $$
A relaxed eatery that offers fresh seafood served with a Southern twist. Favorites include: Crab Shack Famous Deviled Crabs and Smothered Spicy Fried Grouper. 3 locations.

GAULART & MALICLET / FAST & FRENCH
98 Broad St, 843-577-9797
https://fastandfrenchcharleston.com/
CUISINE: French-American

DRINKS: Beer & Wine
SERVING: Breakfast, Lunch & Dinner; Closed Sundays
PRICE RANGE: $$
Small place on Broad with a cozy intimate bar and a communal high-top table is setting for this busy café with a menu mostly of sandwiches, soups and salads. Bar-style seating. Creative French offerings like Turkey and Brie on a French baguette. I always get the daily special, which when I was there was a Hearty Beef Stew with Chèvre, Baguette, Fresh Fruit & a Glass of French Wine, all for one low price. (I also got the soup, which was the Seafood Chowder, though they have 3 or 4 soups to choose from.)

GLASS ONION
1219 Savannah Hwy, Charleston, 843-225-1717
www.ilovetheglassonion.com
CUISINE: Southern
DRINKS: Beer & Wine Only
SERVING: Lunch & Dinner; closed Sun
PRICE RANGE: $$$

Popular upbeat eatery offering a menu of locally sourced Southern fare. Menu picks: Fried quail and Fried NC Trout with Grits and Bacon Braised Turnips. Great desserts like Bread pudding and Crème Brulee. Green wine list.

GOAT SHEEP COW
106 Church St, 843-480-2526
804 Meeting St, 843-203-3118
www.goatsheepcow.com
CUISINE: Cheese & Wine Shop
DRINKS: Wine Bar
SERVING: Lunch & Dinner, Closed Sundays
PRICE RANGE: $$
NEIGHBORHOOD: Downtown
Chic European-style wine bar and cheese shop with old red brick interior, a red leather-style tufted banquette against one wall, a very spacious bar area. Menu with sandwich specials, soups and salads like the Ratatouille Tart, the Chicken Pot Pie, a Daily quiche, charcuterie boards. Fabulous selection of cheeses, of course. Impressive wine list. Patio seating. Wine specials.

GRILL 225
Market Pavilion Hotel
225 E Bay St, Charleston, 843-723-0500
www.grill225.com
CUISINE: Steakhouses
DRINKS: Full Bar
SERVING: Lunch & Dinner
PRICE RANGE: $$$$

One of the best steakhouses in town. It's got the steakhouse "look" down pat. Dark paneled walls rising to a coffered ceiling with impressive moldings, handsome paintings adorning the walls, circular booths against the wall, arched windows looking out into the busy street outside the Market Pavilion Hotel. It's got the usual suspects on the menu, with prices equal to what you'd spend in Miami on South Beach or New York. Any number of cuts of prime steak, Maine lobsters, lots of excellent seafood starters (oysters, scallops, etc.)

THE GROCERY
4 Cannon St, Charleston, 843-302-8825
www.thegrocerycharleston.com
CUISINE: American
DRINKS: Full Bar
SERVING: Dinner; open also for Lunch on Sun, closed Mon
PRICE RANGE: $$$
Comfortable eatery that features Chef Kevin Johnson's seasonal menu made with local and regional ingredients. Favorites include: Warm pear salad, Black Bass, and Roasted Duck Breast. Nice selection of beers and wine. One of the better brunches in town. (I'm a fan of their spicy bloody Mary.)

GULLAH GRUB
877 Sea Island Pkwy, Saint Helena Island, 843-838-3841
www.gullahgrub.com
CUISINE: Seafood/Barbecue
DRINKS: No Booze
SERVING: Lunch & Dinner; Lunch only on Sun, closed Sat
PRICE RANGE: $$
Restaurant with a rustic general store feel offering regional Low Country cuisine. Menu favorites include: Fried Shark Strips with potato salad and BBQ Ribs.

HALL'S CHOPHOUSE
434 King St, 843-727-0090
www.hallschophouse.com
CUISINE: Steakhouse, Seafood
DRINKS: Full Bar
SERVING: Dinner, Lunch & Dinner on Sat & Sun.
PRICE RANGE: $$$$
NEIGHBORHOOD: Radcliffeborough
Red brick walls, white tablecloth service, subdued lighting, a piano player tinkling away against the far wall, interesting artwork adorning the walls—all this sets the scene in this elegant eatery offering a menu of sizeable cuts of beef and seafood specialties (but stick with the excellent selection of beef). Favorites: Dry aged ribeye and Lamb chops Vegetarian options. As a side, get the cornmeal-fried okra or the pepper jack creamed corn. Reservations recommended. Sunday gospel brunch. Has a very lively bar scene, which gives the place a little more jump than you expect in a standard steakhouse. Which is very nice. The bar makes this a great place for lunch. You get the high quality of fine food in an unstuffy atmosphere.

HANK'S SEAFOOD RESTAURANT
10 Hayne St, Charleston, 843-723-3474
www.hanksseafoodrestaurant.com
CUISINE: Seafood
DRINKS: Full Bar
SERVING: Dinner; open nightly
PRICE RANGE: $$$
Located in a turn-of-the-century warehouse overlooking the City Market, this very popular restaurant and bar offers a great selection of seafood

and raw-bar selections. Popular choices include the Seafood a la Wando and Curried Shrimp.

HANNIBAL'S KITCHEN
16 Blake St, 843-722-2256
www.hannibalkitchen.com
CUISINE: Barbecue, American Traditional
DRINKS: No Booze
SERVING: Breakfast, Lunch & Dinner, Closed Sundays
PRICE RANGE: $
NEIGHBORHOOD: East Side
Family-owned eatery known for their Southern seafood specialties in a simple place with no noticeable décor to speak of but also with no pretension. You'll find a lot of places in the Low Country serving shrimp and grits, but the version they have here is one of the best I've encountered. Favorites: Fried chicken with mac & fries; Smothered Liver & Onions; I grew up on fried pork chops and never see them on a menu anymore—here they are wonderful; they have daily specials, and my favorite is the stewed gizzards; Grilled Whiting.

HENRIETTA'S
The Dewberry Hotel
334 Meeting St, Charleston, 843-872-9065
www.henriettascharleston.com
CUISINE: American (New)
DRINKS: Beer & Wine Only
SERVING: Lunch & Dinner
PRICE RANGE: $$
NEIGHBORHOOD: Mazyck-Wraggborough

Located in the Dewberry Hotel, this stylish eatery offers French cuisine with a Southern twist. Also, there's a wonderful raw bar with pickled shrimp and crab Louie. Favorites: Parisian Gnocchi with blue crab and Steak tartare.

HIGH COTTON
199 E Bay St, Charleston, 843-724-3815
www.highcottoncharleston.com
CUISINE: American, Southern
DRINKS: Full bar
SERVING: Dinner daily, Sat lunch, and Sun brunch
PRICE RANGE: $$$
The dining rooms have heart pine floors and antique brick, a perfect setting for their excellent Southern food.

HUSK
74-76 Queen St, Charleston, 843-577-2500
www.huskrestaurant.com
CUISINE: Southern American, Seafood
DRINKS: Full Bar
SERVING: Lunch & Dinner
PRICE RANGE: $$$

Book a table (weeks in advance) in this elegant 19th Century mansion that is the house that Chef Sean Brock built. It's easier to get a table at lunch, and the Husk Cheeseburger is on the menu. You used to have to order the fried chicken 24 hours ahead, but if not, get it. It may be the best fried chicken you ever ate. Cornmeal-dusted catfish from N.C., wood-fired clams from nearby McClellanville. But these are just the beginning of the wonders you'll discover at this award-winning eatery. Brock says, "The secret to good food is good dirt and plant varieties," and he has worked long and hard to bring back heritage seeds used to grow the food he serves here. I could go on and on about this guy, but just make this a must-visit on your trip to the Holy City.

JESTINE'S KITCHEN
251 Meeting St, Charleston, 843-722-7224
www.jestineskitchen.com
CUISINE: Southern
DRINKS: No Booze
SERVING: Lunch & Dinner; closed Mondays
PRICE RANGE: $$

This old-school restaurant offers a menu of Southern classics like Fried chicken and Gumbo. Great desserts like Banana Pudding and Coca Cola cake.

KAMINSKY'S MOST EXCELLENT CAFÉ
78 N Market St, Charleston, 843-853-8270
www.kaminskys.com
CUISINE: Desserts
DRINKS: Full Bar
SERVING: Afternoon-Late night
PRICE RANGE: $$,
The desserts here are prepared fresh daily by the talented pasty chefs who offer a new selection every day. Great menu of specialty coffees, milkshakes (some made with brandy or kahlua) and dessert martinis.

LE FARFALLE
15 Beaufain St, 843-212-0920
www.lefarfallecharleston.com
CUISINE: Italian

DRINKS: Full Bar
SERVING: Lunch & Dinner
PRICE RANGE: $$
NEIGHBORHOOD: Harleston Village, Downtown
The white tablecloths add a touch of elegance to what is a pretty bare room with hard wood floors and an industrial style ceiling. Outdoor patio at night especially is a romantic setting under a big tree providing a spacious canopy. Lively bar scene makes this neighborhood eatery quite popular. The raw bar is basic, but covers what you need: good oysters, lump crab meat, a different crudo every night. They offer mostly Italian fare, creatively imagined, expertly prepared. Housemade pastas. Favorites: Octopus Carpaccio; Polpette (pork meatballs alla Siciliana); a good starter would be the Umbian style stewed chickpeas—interesting flavors at work here; the Pork Chop from their Hogs City supplier is done with caramelized fennel; the Veal Chop is smoked in hay, of all things, imparting a singular taste, and the pureed potatoes only add to the flavorful mix; and the Whipped Ricotta. Weekend brunch. Extensive wine list.

LEON'S OYSTER SHOP
LEON'S FINE POULTRY & OYSTERS
698 King St, Charleston, 843-531-6500
www.leonsoystershop.com
CUISINE: Seafood/Southern
DRINKS: Beer & Wine Only
SERVING: Lunch & Dinner
PRICE RANGE: $$$

This locals' hangout in a cleverly reclaimed former auto body shop downtown offers a creative menu of Southern fare. The oysters can be had raw, fried, char-grilled or Rockefeller. The

chef also has "updated Southern picnic sides" like cole slaw made with yogurt instead of mayo. Other standouts: Leon's Fried Chicken that is cooked to order and the Black-eyed pea salad. There's only one dessert: soft-serve ice cream. The owner, curiously enough, made his name as a star bartender at **FIG**, but here he only serves beer & wine.

LEWIS BARBECUE
464 North Nassau St, 843-805-9500
www.lewisbarbecue.com
CUISINE: Barbecue
DRINKS: Full Bar
SERVING: Lunch & Dinner

PRICE RANGE: $$
NEIGHBORHOOD: NoMo
Popular BBQ eatery serving up Texas-style house-smoked meats. Some of the counters are made with reclaimed wood that has a distressed look. The stripped-down look of the place means the emphasis is on the food. I had a look at the HUGE smokers in the back. Very impressive, but what they turn out is even more impressive. Favorites: Prime Beef Brisket and Pulled pork. Daily specials—I was there on a Wednesday when it was a Barbecue Reuben made with pastrami they cured right here in house. Delicious. Counter service. Outdoor seating available.

LITTLE JACK'S TAVERN
710 King St, 843-531-6868
www.littlejackstavern.com
CUISINE: American Traditional
DRINKS: Full Bar
SERVING: Lunch & Dinner
PRICE RANGE: $$
NEIGHBORHOOD: Downtown
Checkered tablecloths set the tone in this classic American tavern offering a menu of steaks, salads & sandwiches. Has a long spacious bar which makes a great place to have lunch. Classic cocktails. If you're new, try the Garlic knots if you don't mind overdoing it on the carbs. The Tavern burger is a big favorite, but I usually opt in for the Brick Chicken (half a roasted chicken). Has a little crisp to it but lots of flavorful juices.

LOST DOG CAFÉ
106 West Huron Ave, Folly Beach, 843-588-9669
www.lostdogfollybeach.com
CUISINE: American
DRINKS: Full Bar
SERVING: Breakfast & Lunch; open daily
PRICE RANGE: $$
A popular inviting café that serves breakfast all day and a great selection of sandwiches, wraps and salads. Bloody Mary (served in a mason jar) and Folly Eggs Benedict was perfect choice for breakfast.

THE MACINTOSH
4798 King St, Charleston, 843-789-4299
www.themacintoshcharleston.com
CUISINE: American (New)
DRINKS: Full Bar
SERVING: Dinner nightly, lunch on Sun
PRICE RANGE: $$$
A farm-to-table eatery that offers a creative menu of homegrown cuisine prepared by a guy who worked in New York's Per Se and Le Bernardin before coming back to his home town. Though this is really just a tavern, you've never had "tavern" food like this before, I guarantee it. Menu picks include: Pork Shoulder and Bone Marrow bread pudding.

MAGNOLIAS
185 E Bay St, Charleston, 843-577-7771
www.magnoliascharleston.com
CUISINE: Southern
DRINKS: Full Bar
SERVING: Lunch & Dinner
PRICE RANGE: $$$
CUISINE: Southern
DRINKS: Full bar
SERVING: Mon – Sat lunch, Dinner nightly, and Sun brunch
PRICE RANGE: $$$

Magnolias ignited a culinary renaissance when it opened in 1990, paving the way for countless other restaurants across the South. Today, led by executive chef Donald Drake and his team, Magnolias remains a forerunner in upscale Southern cuisine, blending traditional ingredients and cooking techniques with modern flair for artful presentations.

The soul of the South meets the spark of innovation in dishes such as the Down South Egg Roll stuffed with collard greens, chicken, and Tasso ham, served with red pepper purée, spicy mustard sauce, and peach chutney and Shellfish over Grits with sautéed shrimp, sea scallops, lobster, creamy white grits, lobster butter sauce and fried spinach.

MARTHA LOU'S KITCHEN
1068 Morrison Dr., Charleston, 843-577-9583
www.marthalouskitchen.com
CUISINE: Southern; soul food
DRINKS: No booze
SERVING: Breakfast, lunch (closes at 5)
PRICE RANGE: $
Unpretentious place where Martha Lou Gadsden has been cooking for decades. If she's not there, her daughters will be. Excellent fried chicken, but I always pass it up (too many gourmet cooks around the country are making some pretty good fried chicken, so you can get it anywhere) and opt for the smothered pork chops (a dish those fancy chefs

haven't mastered yet or are too proud to cook), green beans cooked almost to a delicious mush, or try the fried whiting over grits. Heavenly food for someone like me who grew up not far from here. I draw the line at chitlins (chitterlings), but if you want them, you can get them here at this gritty, wonderful, iconic place.

McCRADY'S
155 E. Bay St, 843-577-0025
www.mccradysrestaurant.com
CUISINE: American
DRINKS: Full bar
SERVING: Dinner daily
PRICE RANGE: $$$$
McCrady's Restaurant, which is listed on the National Register of Historic Places and Landmarks, represents the best of the amalgam that is new Southern fine dining, serving as a canvas for postmodern gastronomy. The menu, created by Chef Sean Brock,

2010 James Beard Best Chef Southeast award-winner, centers around inventive cuisine fresh from the farm and local purveyors. McCrady's bar specializes in hand-crafted cocktails and features a Wine Spectator Award-winning wine list, as well as a diverse and delicious Bar Snack menu created by Chef Brock. Each day, a chalkboard above the bar offers several featured snacks.

MERCANTILE AND MASH
701 E Bay St, Charleston, 843-793-2636
www.mercandmash.com
CUISINE: American (Traditional)/Desserts
DRINKS: No Booze
SERVING: Breakfast, Lunch & Dinner
PRICE RANGE: $$
NEIGHBORHOOD: Eastside
Very absorbing space located in an old warehouse that seems a combination of restaurant, meat store, craft store and gift shop. Here you'll also find baked goods, specialty foods, cheeses, beer and wine. Great choice for Sunday Brunch. Dine-in or take-out. Great fun just to browse.

MINERO
153B E Bay St, Charleston, 843-789-2241
www.minerorestaurant.com
CUISINE: Mexican
DRINKS: Full Bar
SERVING: Lunch & Dinner
PRICE RANGE: $$
NEIGHBORHOOD: French Quarter

Popular Mexican eatery with a gorgeous bar and booths for dining. Famed **Husk** Chef Sean Brock is behind this casual spot that's a big hit. As in his other restaurants, the ingredients here are all heirloom, from the beans to the pork to the peppers. It's actually better Mexican food than the Mexicans make because they don't start off with ingredients this good. Mexican favorites: Chilaquiles, grilled steak tacos, and guacamole and special dishes like fish tacos. Try the blended Satanico – their house drink.

MUSE RESTAURANT AND WINE BAR
82 Society St., 843-577-1102
www.charlestonmuse.com
CUISINE: American, Italian, Mediterranean
DRINKS: Full bar
SERVING: Dinner daily
PRICE RANGE: $$$

There are 100 wine offerings by the glass and 500 bottle offerings from producers all around the world, who create products that are true to their region, history, and varietal. The menu offers dishes inspired by the many cultures of the Mediterranean and is prepared with local ingredients.

NANA'S SEAFOOD & SOUL
176 Line St, Charleston, 843-937-0002
www.nanasseafoodsoul.com
CUISINE: Soul Food
DRINKS: No Booze
SERVING: Lunch & Dinner (close early)
PRICE RANGE: $$
NEIGHBORHOOD: Jonestown
Small eatery known for its menu of authentic soul food. Specials change daily but the chef utilizes local ingredients including the seafood, which is why you can only get shrimp & grits when they have freshly caught shrimp. Speaking of shrimp, you're going to love their shrimp: after being perfectly cooked, the shrimp are slathered with a brown sauce made of yellow, red and orange peppers, sausage and bacon. Also tops are the deviled crabs and the "chewies," brownies stuffed with pecans. They only have 3 tables, so this is mostly a take-out place.

THE OBSTINATE DAUGHTER
2063 Middle St, Sullivan's Island, 843-416-5020
www.theobstinatedaughter.com
CUISINE: Pizza, Seafood, Mediterranean
DRINKS: Full Bar
SERVING: Lunch & Dinner
PRICE RANGE: $$
NEIGHBORHOOD: Sullivan's Island
A chic rustic eatery that pays homage to the rich history of Sullivan's Island, the walls are made with gorgeous reclaimed wood with loads of texture and charm. Menu features a nice mixture of seafood and Mediterranean dishes. Favorites include: Frogmore Chowder and Bucatini Carbonara. The pizzas from

the wood-fired ovens are made with flour from heritage-grain champ Anson Mills. Nice desserts like their N.C. apple bread pudding and red velvet cake.

THE ORDINARY
544 King St, Charleston, 843-414-7060
www.eattheordinary.com
CUISINE: Seafood, Sandwiches; Southern
DRINKS: Full Bar
SERVING: Dinner
PRICE RANGE: $$$
Set in an old bank building from 1927, this spot has a striking décor with high ceilings and large arched windows. By the old bank vault you'll see the big raw

bar stacked high with clams, oysters and crabs. (Try the pickled shrimp.) Labeled as an American brasserie and Oyster Hall, this eatery offers Chef Mike Lata's take on Southern seafood. Menu favorites include: Lobster Roll, swordfish schnitzel, Black Bass Provencal, and Peekytoe Crab Louie. Best experience is to share lots of small plates. Desserts offered include the delicious Carolina Rice Pudding with Peaches and Figs.

THE PARK CAFÉ
730 Rutledge Ave, Charleston, 843-410-1070
www.theparkcafechs.com
CUISINE: American (New)/Seafood
DRINKS: Full Bar
SERVING: Breakfast, Lunch & Dinner
PRICE RANGE: $$
NEIGHBORHOOD: Wagener Terrace
Popular neighborhood café serving American fare in a comfy room. Farm to table seasonal menu with favorites like Egg bacon ravioli and Veggies Mess (a delicious vegetable entrée). Daily Specials. Great wine list.

PEARLZ OYSTER BAR
153 East Bay St, Charleston, 843-577-5755
www.pearlzoysterbar.com
CUISINE: Seafood
DRINKS: Full Bar
SERVING: Dinner
PRICE RANGE: $$
Located in the heart of the historic district, this eclectic seafood eatery is a great way to experience

Charleston. Menu favorites include: Blackened Mahi Mahi over cheddar grits and Tuna Tartar. Creative desserts. No reservations. Sometimes a wait.

PENINSULA GRILL
Planter's Inn
112 N Market St, Charleston, 843-723-0700
www.peninsulagrill.com
CUISINE: American (New)/Steakhouse
DRINKS: Full Bar
SERVING: Dinner nightly
PRICE RANGE: $$$$
When you stroll up the red brick walkway meandering through a lushly landscape courtyard, you know you're in for something special. Posh eatery (velvet walls) with a creative menu of upscale Southern fare. A recent starter I loved was Lobster Skillet Cake & Crab Cake Duo with Smoked Bacon-Parsley Salad and Creamed Corn. I followed it with pan-seared Carolina trout with blue crab and capers. (Menu is seasonal, so it changes.) Where else can you get a slice of coconut cake that's 12 layers high? This cake is so famous they will even ship it to you by overnight express (for $130). I admit I never tasted it. (I always get the orange vanilla cheesecake.) Insist on a table outside in the courtyard if the weather suits.

POOGAN'S PORCH RESTAURANT
72 Queen St., 843-577-2337
www.poogansporch.com
CUISINE: Southern
DRINKS: Full bar
SERVING: Lunch and dinner daily, brunch Sat - Sun
PRICE RANGE: $$

Tucked away on charming Queen Street, Poogan's Porch is one of Charleston's oldest independent culinary establishments, with a fresh approach to Lowcountry cuisine. Recognized by Martha Stewart Living, Wine Spectator and The Travel Channel, this beautifully restored Victorian house is the perfect southern spot for lunch, dinner or weekend brunch. Since opening in 1976, Poogan's Porch has been a favorite of well-known celebrities, politicians, tourists and locals alike who rave about this Southern institution. Whether it's a warm homemade buttermilk biscuit and sausage gravy for brunch, a bowl of she-crab soup for lunch, or our signature buttermilk fried chicken for dinner, your meal at Poogan's will be unforgettable. A state-of-the-art, 1500-bottle wine cellar and over 28 wines offered by the glass will be a perfect complement to any meal.

PURLIEU
237 Fishburne St, 843-300-2253
www.purlieucharleston.com
CUISINE: French
DRINKS: Wine Bar
SERVING: Dinner, Closed Sun & Mon.
PRICE RANGE: $$$
NEIGHBORHOOD: Westside
Casual bistro atmosphere enhanced by the slated wood ceiling gives this French place a welcoming feel. Small, and even cramped when it gets busy, but that's not a negative. I liked it that way. They have a creative menu featuring bouillabaisse, duck prosciutto & fusion French cuisine. Favorites: Hanger Steak and Frog Legs with puff pastry. Save room for the 100-layer Chocolate cake. Reservations recommended.

RENZO
384 Huger St, 843-952-7864
www.renzochs.com
CUISINE: Pizza, Italian
DRINKS: Wine Bar
SERVING: Dinner, Lunch & Dinner on Sundays, Closed Mondays
PRICE RANGE: $$$
NEIGHBORHOOD: Downtown
Popular upscale eatery in a long narrow room with a friendly bar on one side complemented with booths

against the other wall – they have really tasty wood-fired Neapolitan pizza—a large selection, like and Wrath of Kahan pizza (piquillo pepper sauce, chorizo, medjool dates) and other fare, like Wood-fired Eggplant and Lo Mein Carbonara. Extensive wine list.

RITA'S SEASIDE GRILLE
2 Center St, Folly Beach, 843-588-2525
www.ritasseasidegrille.com
CUISINE: Burgers/Seafood
DRINKS: Full Bar
SERVING: Breakfast, Lunch & Dinner
PRICE RANGE: $$
NEIGHBORHOOD: Folly Beach
A fun spot located just steps from the beach and the Folly Fishing Pier. Menu is typical American fare of burgers and seafood. Favorites include the award-winning Rita's Chili.

RODNEY SCOTT'S BBQ
1011 King St, 843-990-9535
www.rodneyscottsbbq.com
Website down at press time
CUISINE: Barbecue
DRINKS: Full Bar
SERVING: Lunch & Dinner
PRICE RANGE: $$
NEIGHBORHOOD: North Central
Popular counter-serve eatery offering Low Country-style smoked pulled pork BBQ, chicken and ribs. Has a big to-go business, but there are a few booths and other tables if you want to eat here. Outside, they

have some picnic tables where you can also eat, with the wood they use to smoke their meats stacked high between the tables. Favorites: Southern-fried catfish and Smoked Turkey.

THE ROOFTOP
19 Vendue Range, Charleston, 843-577-7970
www.thevendue.com/charleston-dining/the-rooftop
CUISINE: American (Traditional)/Lounge
DRINKS: Full Bar
SERVING: Lunch & Dinner
PRICE RANGE: $$
NEIGHBORHOOD: French Quarter
Located on the rooftop of the **Vendue Hotel**, this place is great as a meeting spot for lunch. From this vantage point you get a great view of the church steeples that puncture the city's skyline, as well a super good view of the harbor. Excellent at happy hour for a sunset you'll remember. Favorites: Pulled Pork Nachos and Signature Lobster Rolls. Extensive cocktail menu. Great views.

RUTLEDGE CAB CO
1300 Rutledge Ave, Charleston, 843-720-1440
www.rutledgecabco.com
CUISINE: American (New), Burgers
DRINKS: Full Bar
SERVING: Lunch & Dinner
PRICE RANGE: $$
Located in a former convenience store/gas station, this popular eatery offers a menu of American comfort food. Many of the menu favorites are cooked over Charleston's only indoor charcoal grill. Indoor and outdoor seating.

SECOND STATE COFFEE
70 1/2 Beaufain St, Charleston, 843-793-4402
https://secondstatecoffee.com
CUISINE: Coffee & Tea
DRINKS: Full Bar
SERVING: 7 a.m. – 7 p.m.
PRICE RANGE: $$
A minimalist coffee bar that offers coffees, beverages, and a variety of pastries.
Free Wi-Fi.

THE SHELLMORE
357 N Shelmore Blvd, 843-654-9278
www.theshellmore.com
CUISINE: Seafood
DRINKS: Wine Bar
SERVING: Dinner, Closed Sun & Mon.
NEIGHBORHOOD: Mount Pleasant
Cozy eatery featuring a wine and raw bar, which is why I come here—the OYSTERS, which are among

the plumpest, juiciest I've had in Charleston. There is big horseshoe-shaped bar inside and some pleasant outdoor seating as well. Menu changes daily – mostly sandwiches and small plates. Favorites: Charred octopus; Country Paté, Beef & Pork Ragu over capunti pasta.

STARS ROOFTOP & GRILL ROOM
495 King St, Charleston, 843-577-0100
www.starsrestaurant.com
CUISINE: American/Steakhouse
DRINKS: Full Bar
SERVING: Dinner nightly, Lunch on weekends
PRICE RANGE: $$$
Located in the historic district, this stunning 1930's style Grill Room and Walnut Bar offers a seasonal menu of steaks and regional dishes – shared and large places. Menu favorites include: Grass fed NC Bone-in Rib eye and Lobster & Grits. For a treat reserve a seat

at the Chef's Table (seats 12) for a top-notch dining experience.

THE SWAMP FOX
Francis Marion Hotel
387 King St, Charleston, 843-724-8888
www.francismarionhotel.com/
CUISINE: American (New)/Southern
DRINKS: Full Bar
SERVING: Breakfast, Lunch & Dinner
PRICE RANGE: $$
Located in the historic Francis Marion Hotel, this popular eatery (originally opened in 1924) offers a revolving menu of regional specialties inspired by the Old South. Award-wining shrimp & grits served with a white lobster-based gravy and topped off with orange peppers, scallions and bits of smoked Tasso ham. The grits themselves come from an historic Columbia mill named Adluh. (Get the appetizer portion instead of the main course just so you can taste this great dish.) Live jazz piano on weekends.

TACO BOY
217 Huger St, Charleston, 843-789-3333
www.tacoboy.net
CUISINE: Mexican
DRINKS: Full Bar
SERVING: Lunch & Dinner
PRICE RANGE: $$
An authentic Taqueria/Cantina that offers a creative menu of Mexican fare featuring tacos with innovative fillings. Great frozen cocktails. Indoor and outdoor seating.

TATTOOED MOOSE
1137 Morrison Dr, 843-277-2990
www.tattooedmoose.com
CUISINE: American Traditional
DRINKS: Full Bar
SERVING: Lunch & Dinner
PRICE RANGE: $$
NEIGHBORHOOD: Downtown

Popular neighborhood spot serving upscale bar food & sandwiches. There's a big dead moose head hanging over the bar, so hunters will feel especially welcome. Lots of other dead critters, like a beaver, or parts of dead critters, a couple of antlers, a cow's skull, decorating the walls. Graffiti is everywhere, and I mean everywhere. It's your dream idea of a dive bar atmosphere. A couple of pinball machines. A favorite is the Duck Club served with Duck fat fries. Lots of other very tasty bar grub. Craft beers.

VIRGINIA'S ON KING
412 King St, Charleston, 843-735-5800
www.holycityhospitality.com/virginias-on-king
CUISINE: Southern
DRINKS: Beer & Wine Only
SERVING: Breakfast, Lunch & Dinner
PRICE RANGE: $$
This upscale favorite is known for its Southern comfort food dishes made from old family recipes (even their fried pickles). Menu favorites include: blackened catfish, fried chicken, she-crab soup and the Lowcountry Boil, a hearty stew containing sausage, potatoes, corn and shrimp. Their key lime pie is a standout.

WILD OLIVE RESTAURANT
2867 Maybank Hwy, Johns Island, 843-737-4177
www.wildoliverestaurant.com
CUISINE: Italian
DRINKS: Full Bar
SERVING: Lunch & Dinner

PRICE RANGE: $$
NEIGHBORHOOD: John's Island
A friendly eatery with a rustic-chic vibe that offers a simple menu of Italian fare. Portions are large and the food is good. Favorites include: Short Ribs and Calamari Napoletano. Nice wine list. First certified green restaurant in S.C.

WORKMEN'S CAFÉ
1837 N Grimball Rd, 843-406-0120
No Website
CUISINE: Seafood / Soul Food / Southern
DRINKS: No Booze
SERVING: Lunch 11-4 (till 6 on Fri); Closed Sat, Sun & Mon.
PRICE RANGE: $
NEIGHBORHOOD: James Island
Very, very reasonably-priced cafeteria style eatery serving seafood, soul food and Southern specialties. Favorites: Pork chops; Country fried steak; Okra; Red rice, BBQ. Damn, it's ALL good.

WORKSHOP
1503 King St, 843-996-4500
www.workshopcharleston.com
CUISINE: Food Court
DRINKS: Full Bar
SERVING: Lunch & Dinner. Brunch on weekends.
PRICE RANGE: $$
NEIGHBORHOOD: Wagener Terrace
Trendy food court offering a rotating roster of chefs. Everything from Hanger steak to Spring rolls and

Sushi. Cafeteria style. Here are some of the stations / stalls as we were going to press:

LITTLE MISS HA
https://www.workshopcharleston.com/kitchens/little-miss-ha

SUSHI WA IZAKAYA
https://www.workshopcharleston.com/kitchens/sushi-wa-izakaya

MERROWS GARDEN BAR
https://www.workshopcharleston.com/kitchens/merrows-garden-bar

FREE REIGN
https://www.workshopcharleston.com/kitchens/free-reign

REBEL TAQUERIA
https://www.workshopcharleston.com/kitchens/rebel-taqueria

CHICK & PATTY'S
https://www.workshopcharleston.com/kitchens/chuck-pattys

CAFÉ ROUX
https://www.workshopcharleston.com/kitchens/cafe-roux

WRECK OF THE RICHARD & CHARLENE
106 Haddrell St, 843-884-0052
www.wreckrc.com
DRINKS: Beer & Wine
SERVING: Dinner from 5, but closed Monday
PRICE RANGE: $$
NEIGHBORHOOD: Mount Pleasant
Simple eatery that has to be one of the most picturesque you'll find anywhere, as it overlooks a working marina. Sit outside (or inside) and look out over some real working fishing boats and saltwater marshes. There are still some wetlands wading birds that show up. Get a look at this scene now—it won't be here forever. This is a locals' favorite serving Low Country-style fried seafood. What I love about this place is that there are no concessions to "landlubbers." The food here is strictly seafood, and most of that is fried, fried, fried. (But you can still get broiled and grilled items.) Favorites: Grilled scallops; Fried oysters, Deviled crab and definitely the Hush puppies. Just get the Seafood Platter and be done with it. Paper plates and menus here. Just circle your choice with a red marker. Desserts are homemade, and my favorite is the Key Lime Bread Pudding. No reservations, no a/c (a screened in porch), no cell phone use in dining room (you have to go outside). Good for them! At least they take credit cards, LOL.

XIAO BAO BISCUIT
224 Rutledge Ave, Charleston, No Phone
www.xiaobaobiscuit.com
CUISINE: Vietnamese, Japanese, Taiwanese
DRINKS: Full Bar
SERVING: Lunch & Dinner daily; closed Sunday
PRICE RANGE: $$$
Located in a converted gas station, this trendy multicultural eatery offers a menu of Asian comfort food. Vegan/Vegetarian/Gluten-free options available. Specialty cocktails.

ZERO RESTAURANT + BAR
0 George St, 843-817-7900
www.zerogeorge.com - for hotel
https://zerorestaurantcharleston.com/ - for restaurant
CUISINE: American (New)

DRINKS: Full Bar
SERVING: Dinner, Closed Mondays
PRICE RANGE: $$$
NEIGHBORHOOD: East Side, NoMo
Located in the restored 1804 **Zero George Street Hotel**, this unique café offers award-winning cuisine in a very Colonial setting within the hotel that's made up on 3 historic houses and a courtyard. Very elegant, very romantic, very charming. It's nice to slip in to have a drink at the tiny little bar or sit out on the verandah. There's a chef's tasting menu available, and this changes all the time, so not sure wht you'll get the night you visit. Favorites: Beef Wellington and Scallop Tartare. Vegetarian options available. Classic cocktails. There's also a happy hour and a small Bar Menu (things like Lobster Rolls, Deviled Eggs, Charcuterie Board).

Chapter 5
NIGHTLIFE

Charleston is not particularly known for its night life — the options sometimes come down to one outlandishly named martini versus another (caramel macchiatotini? Charlestoniantini?). But locals with an evening to kill stop by the lounge of their choice.

BIN 152
152 King St, Charleston, 843-577-7359
www.bin152.com
Bin 152 is known as Charleston's best wine bar (with hints of France in its décor of marble-topped café tables and wainscoting, but there are communal tables also), but it's also a cheese bar, art gallery and

antiques market. Located in the French Quarter, BIN 152 offers 30 different wines by the glass and over 130 wines by the bottle. They serve over 40 different cheeses and charcuteries with freshly baked bread.

COCKTAIL CLUB
479 King St #200, Charleston, 843-724-9411
www.thecocktailclubcharleston.com/
Located above **The Macintosh**, this upscale lounge celebrates the craft cocktail. If you're into creative cocktails stop here and sample one of their house-made infusions or rare liquors. Three lounge areas including a rooftop terrace and custom garden. Menu of light fare available. Live music.

CLOSED FOR BUSINESS
453 King St, Charleston, 843-853-8466
www.closed4business.com
This popular bar offers the "most eclectic draught beer selection in the Southeast." They certainly back up that claim with forty-two taps and featuring Charleston's best rare and one-of-a-kind beers. Bar snacks available.

.
THE GIN JOINT
182 E Bay St, Charleston, 843-577-6111
www.theginjoint.com
The Gin Joint serves quality pre-prohibition style cocktails made from locally sourced herbs, house made syrups, and top tier booze. Great drink menu and wonderful soft pretzels.

THE GRIFFON
18 Vendue Range St, Charleston, 843-723-1700
www.griffoncharleston.com
This English Pub was voted "Best Bar in the South" by *Southern Living*. Located in the historic district, this popular hangout offers local brews on tap, several TVs, and friendly staff.

MYNT
135 Calhoun St, Charleston, 843-718-1598
www.myntcharleston.com
Mynt is a popular new bar/club with a great innovative design catering to the young professionals. Mynt offers great variety of cocktails and appetizers. Weekends are busy so be prepared to wait in line.

PAVILION BAR AT THE MARKET PAVILION HOTEL
225 E Bay St, Charleston, 843-723-0500
www.marketpavilion.com/pavilionbar.cfm

This place makes a perfect stop for a nightcap before turning in. From the rooftop bar you can look out over the church steeples and into the waters of the Ashley river pulsing by. Off to your north you'll see the lighted Ravenel Bridge soaring over the U.S.S. Yorktown Museum.

VOODOO TIKI BAR
15 Magnolia Rd, Charleston, 843-769-0228
www.voodootikibar.com
Voodoo Tiki Bar & Lounge serves a great selection of cocktails including Tequilas & Sakes. A fun place with a creative bar menu and friendly staff. Duck sliders are a favorite. Drink specials.

Chapter 6
WHAT TO SEE & DO

ANGEL OAK
3688 Angel Oak Rd, Charleston, 843-559-3496
www.angeloaktree.com
This tree is so large it will baffle you. It's between 300 and 400 years old. The gate in the fence around it closes at 5.

BASICO AT MIXSON BATH & RACQUET CLUB
4401 McCarthy Street, North Charleston, 843-471-1920
www.mixsonbrc.com
This beautifully designed bath & racquet club offers members a place to wear their tennis whites and enjoy poolside dance parties. A place where the hippest stuffed shirt feels at home. The venue boasts a pool house, yoga and wellness space, a 3,200 square ft. heated saltwater pool, nine private cabanas, and a well-appointed clubhouse and restaurant. Mixon Bath is the private side of the place, and is separated from the open-to-the-public part, BASICO (phone is 843-471-1670), where you'll love the margaritas.

THE BATTERY

At the foot of the peninsula is The Battery, lined with majestic antebellum mansions that people still live in. Some have been converted into elegant lodgings, but you'll see that this really is a neighborhood, first and foremost. The Battery overlooks the harbor and Fort Sumter. The best time to come here is in the morning, before all the tourists and families besiege it. Then you can smell the oleander that grows on the edge of the palm-lined promenade.

THE BICYCLE SHOPPE
280 Meeting St, Charleston, 843-722-8168
www.thebicycleshoppecharleston.com
A popular way to see Charleston is by bike. Bicycle Shoppe rents comfortable beach cruisers and even offers route suggestions. Bike along the streets to

view the variety of architectural styles and photograph the charming shady streets.

BOONE HALL PLANTATION
1235 Long Point Road, Mount Pleasant, 843-884-4371
www.boonehallplantation.com
ADMISSION: Moderate admission fee
Open to the public since 1956, this working plantation recently made headlines with actress Blake Lively married actor Ryan Reynolds on the Cotton Dock of the plantation. The plantation features a grand main house and rows of slave quarters. The entry to the plantation is quite spectacular with a nearly mile-long line of 270-year old live oaks covered in Spanish moss.

BULLDOG TOURS
18 Anson St, Charleston, 843-402-722-8687
https://www.bulldogtours.com/
Has a variety of tours of historic Charleston including food tours, history tours, ghost tours—check out the website for current offerings.

CHARLES TOWNE PUB STROLL
78 Broad Street, Charleston, 843-345-9714
www.pubstroll.com/
Not your typical historic tour, this unique tour is not only peppered with true Charleston stories but stops at many of Charleston's favorite pubs. The guide is dressed in period costume and shares historical stories of drinking habits, Prohibition-era criminals and such. The 2 - 3 hour tour includes samplings of libations

from some of the pubs on the tour. Beverages are included in the price of the tour. Reservations necessary.

CHARLESTON CITY MARKET
188 Meeting St, Charleston, 843-937-0920
www.thecharlestoncitymarket.com
Open 364 days per year, this open-air market is a favorite of tourists and locals. There's a huge number of vendors selling a variety of products including: paintings, soaps, pottery, and Charleston's famous sweetgrass baskets. There's also a variety of restaurants from casual to fine dining.

CHARLESTON CULINARY TOURS
21 S Market St, Charleston, 843-259-2966
www.charlestonculinarytours.com
These tours combine the best of Charleston history with great food and drinks while giving an insightful historic tour (there are six different tours – Downtown, Upper King Street, Chef's Showcase at The Farmer's Market, Chef's Kitchen, Mixology and Distillery). On each tour you're able to taste delicious food offerings and often meet the owners of the restaurants. Tours sell out so reservations are a must.

CHARLESTON KAYAK COMPANY
4290 Ashley River Rd, Charleston, 843-628-2879
www.charlestonkayakcompany.com
This Charleston-based kayak company offers tours throughout Coastal South Carolina. Paddle the wide-rage of diverse eco-systems in one of many scheduled daily tours or a private customized guided tour. Available are kayak tours, kayak rentals, or private boat charters to undeveloped beaches.

CHARLESTON STAGE COMPANY
Dock Street Theatre, 135 Church St, Charleston, 843-577-7183
www.charlestonstage.com
Which presents musicals and popular fare the rest of the year (tickets $20 to $52).

CHARLESTON STROLLS
18 Anson St, Charleston, 843-766-2080
www.charlestonstrolls.com **WEBSITE DOWN AT PRESSTIME**
Since 1979, this company has offered walking tours of Charleston's historic district. The company also offers customized tour packages. Learn about

Charleston's unique history while visiting local historic buildings. The Christmas tours are among the best.

COASTAL EXPEDITIONS
514 Mill St, Mount Pleasant, 843-884-7684
www.coastalexpeditions.com
Has three-hour trips for a reasonable fee.

CONGREGATION KAHAL KADOSH BETH ELOHIM
90 Hasell St, Charleston, 843-723-1090
www.kkbe.org
NEIGHBORHOOD: Ansonborough
People don't think of Charleston as an important town for Jews, but it has been for a very long time. An 1840 historical landmark, this synagogue is the second oldest synagogue building in the United States. (The congregation itself dates back to 1749.) Excellent example of Greek Revival architecture. Tours available (4 times daily, 3 times on Sunday, no tours on Saturday – nominal fee). Gift shop.

DOCK STREET THEATRE
135 Church St, Charleston, 843-7577-7183
www.charlestonstage.com
The Dock Street Theater opened in 1736 with a production of "The Recruiting Officer." This masterpiece of Georgian architecture is supposedly the first purpose-built theatre in the U.S. Performances by the **Charleston Stage Theatre Company** – www.charlestonstage.com - and also during **Spoleto**.

DRAYTON HALL
3380 Ashley River Rd, Charleston, 843-769-2600
www.draytonhall.org
HOURS: Open daily
ADMISSION: Moderate priced ticket – includes guided tour
NEIGHBORHOOD: Ashley River
Located about 15 miles northwest of Charleston, this 18th-century plantation is the only one to survive intact both the Revolutionary and Civil wars and the nation's earliest example of fully executed Palladian architecture. This is the oldest example of Georgian Palladian style not just in Charleston, but in the whole country, as it dates back to 1738. When the Drayton family gave the plantation to the National Trust, it was with the stipulation that the house remain as it is, so what they've done is "maintain" it rather than "restore" it. Take the tour and you'll get an eerie feeling that you've gone back in time. Guided and self- tours available.

EDMONDSTON-ALSTON HOUSE
21 E Battery, Charleston, 843-722-7171
www.edmondstonalston.com
HOURS: Open daily
ADMISSION: Minimum fee
Built in 1825 by Scottish shipping merchant Charles Edmonston, this historic Federal-style home revels in its past. Take a short tour of this place to see the incredible architecture, furnishings, paintings, and personal family artifacts on display. From the plaza out front, you have a commanding view of Charleston

Harbor. It was from this vantage point that Confederate General P.G.T. Beauregard observed the shelling of Fort Sumter that ignited the Civil War, or as my 5th Grade teacher called it, the War of Northern Aggression.

FIREFLY DISTILLERY
6775 Bears Bluff Rd, Wadmalaw Island, 843-557-1405
www.fireflyspirits.com/le-gate
 A scenic vineyard about a 30-minute drive from downtown on sleepy Wadmalaw Island. The owners have spent years trying to make muscadine wine without the syrupy, made-at-home sweetness those words bring to Southerners' minds. Two years ago, the owners took on another iconic Southern taste, iced tea, blending it with vodka to make Firefly Sweet Tea Vodka, whose authentic lazy-Sunday-afternoon flavor made it a runaway success. After the free Saturday vineyard tour at 2 p.m., you can taste both.

FORT SUMTER TOURS
340 Concord St. # 201, 843-722-2628

www.fortsumtertours.com
With two departure points: Liberty Square (340 Concord St) and Patriots Point (40 Patriots Pt. Rd., Mt. Pleasant), these tours include a 30-minute narrated cruise to the historic Fort Sumter. Upon arrival, guests are greeted by National Park Service Rangers who share more details about Fort Sumter and its role in the "War Between the States." The fort's museum includes many historic artifacts and a souvenir shop. The Fort Sumter visit lasts an hour before you return on a scenic cruise back to your departure point.

GALLERY CHUMA
188 Meeting St, Charleston, 843-722-1702
www.gallerychuma.com

The Gullah people are descendants of enslaved Africans who settled on isolated sea islands and marshland areas from Jacksonville, Fla., to Wilmington, N.C., in the 19th Century. They live in small farming and fishing communities along the Atlantic coastal plain and on the chain of Sea Islands which runs parallel to the coast. Because of their geographical isolation and strong community life, the Gullah have been able to preserve more of their African cultural heritage than any other group of African Americans. They speak a Creole language similar to Sierra Leone Krio, use African names, tell African folktales, make African-style handicrafts such as baskets and carved walking sticks, and enjoy a rich cuisine based primarily on rice. Today, various factors threaten Gullah communities, including developers seeking land to build resorts and condominiums along with younger generations leaving ancestral Gullah lands for college or employment and not returning.

Gullah Art is a recognized art genre, much like Native American Indian Art. Gullah Art by Indigenous Gullah artists are more than just aesthetics, it is a desire by these artists to preserve their culture and lifestyle that is under attack on many fronts. You'll find all kinds of their art in this gallery.

GATEWAY WALK

One thing Charleston will never have is the sheer number of square lines with stately oaks that Savannah can boast. But Gallery walk is no slouch when it comes to oaks heavy with moss. The 4-block stretch is among the most beautiful things to see in Charleston. there are smaller gardens tucked away and they're all loosely connected. Some of the oldest churches are to be found here, including **St. John's** and **St. Philip's**.

GIBBES MUSEUM OF ART
135 Meeting St, Charleston, 843-722-2706
www.gibbesmuseum.org
ADMISSION: Nominal fee
HOURS: 10 – 5 daily; closed Mon.
NEIGHBORHOOD: French Quarter
One of the oldest arts organizations in the United States. Known for shaping the careers of American artists for over a century. First floor offers studios for art lessons and children's activities. Floors 2 & 3 are reserved for permanent and visiting exhibits.

GRAY LINE TOURS
375 Meeting St, 843-722-4444
www.graylineofcharleston.com
OFFERS 3 TOURS: Historic Charleston; Historic Charleston & Historic Homes; and a Historic Charleston & Fort Sumter Harbor Tour. All are reasonably priced and good.

GULLAH TOURS
375 Meeting St, Charleston, 843-763-7551
www.gullahtours.com
 Led by Alphonso Brown, a lifelong resident who demonstrates his native Gullah tongue. Mr. Brown displays an encyclopedic knowledge of oft-overlooked sites like the Brown Fellowship Graveyard for Light Skinned Blacks (not to be confused with the Thomas Smalls Graveyard for the Society of Freed Blacks of Dark Complexion just next to it). The two-hour tour meets at:

HALSEY INSTITUTE OF CONEMPORARY ART
161 Calhoun St, Charleston, 843-953-4422
http://halsey.cofc.edu/
HOURS: Open Mon – Sat until 4 p.m.
ADMISSION: No Admission fee
This welcome addition to Charleston's somewhat quirky collection of museums is on the campus of the College of Charleston. It doesn't have its own collection, which is why they call places like this "non-collecting museums." Rather, they offer traveling exhibitions of new and established artists from all over the world. They have a media room, reference library, archive, lecture hall, recital hall, two theater spaces and a film screening facility. The institute offers tours, lectures, workshops, and special educational programming. The first thing I do when I arrive in Charleston is check to see what's on the schedule.

THE HUNLEY
1250 Supply St, Charleston, 843-743-4865
www.hunley.org
The H.L. Hunley, a submarine nearly 40 feet long, played a small part in the American Civil War. This vessel was the first combat submarine to sink an enemy warship. Named for the inventor, Horace Lawson Hunley, the submarine was lost for years but was recovered in 2000. Now on display at the Warren Lasch Conservation Center. Weekend tours available for nominal fee.

MAGNOLIA CEMETERY
70 Cunnington Ave, Charleston, 843-722-8638.
www.magnoliacemetery.net
This 92-acre historical cemetery dates back to the 1850s. The cemetery is populated with headstones shaped like pyramids and adorned with angels, and mausoleums that are architectural gems. There's even

a pond with a drawbridge but beware of the alligators. Magnolia Cemetery is one of the best examples of rural and Victorian cemetery design in the US. Makes a good place for a picnic after strolling the landscaped paths and ponds.

MAGNOLIA PLANTATION & GARDENS
3550 Ashley River Rd, Charleston, 843-571-1266
www.magnoliaplantation.com
HOURS: Open daily until 4 p.m.
ADMISSION: Minimal admission fee
Promoted as "Charleston's most visited plantation," the plantation and gardens have received many favorable reviews including "America's Most Beautiful Gardens" rating from Travel + Leisure Magazine. These are probably the oldest public

gardens in America, opening its doors to visitors in 1870.

MIDDLETON PLACE PLANTATION
4300 Ashley River Rd, Charleston, 843-556-6020
www.middletonplace.org
There are a handful of fine restored plantations just a short drive from Charleston. You're missing one of the best experiences by not visiting one of them. At this National Historic Landmark, you'll see the oldest landscaped garden in the U.S. The House Tour (lasts a half-hour, starts at noon) takes you through the guest quarters, the only part of the 1775 main residence to survive. There's an interesting **African-American Focus Tour** (takes an hour) that offers a very blunt introduction to the "slave experience," something other tours tend to ignore or touch lightly on. Also, you can see what the marshes looked like (before most were drained), or in the winter months, the gray and heavy cypress swamp. Be sure to visit the blacksmith and cooper workshops. Extensive formal gardens. They also have **guided Kayaking Tours**. Call 843-628-2879.

MOUNT PLEASANT
www.tompsc.com
This is a little village just outside Charleston that was settled in the 1600s. Worth an hour or so of your time.

MOUNT PLEASANT PRESBYTERIAN CHURCH
302 Hibben St, Charleston (Mt. Pleasant), 843-884-4612
www.mppc.net
Which once housed a school for freed slaves.

NATHANIEL RUSSELL HOUSE
51 Meeting St, Charleston, 843-724-8481
www.historiccharleston.org
HOURS: Open daily until 5 p.m.
ADMISSION: Minimal admission fee
This historic house offers visitors a chance to explore what daily life was like in one of Charleston's most exquisite homes. The interiors are restored to their original 1808 grandeur. Visitors can learn about the history of the family who lived here (Russell was a rich shipping merchant in his day) and the servants who maintained one of the nation's grandest townhouses. It's considered by historians as one of

the more important residences designed in the Neoclassical style. It's big, at some 9,000 square feet. Over the years, this house has been many things, including a boarding school for some 50 years, so it had been through hell by the time the trust decided in 1995 to raise money and do some research to return the house to as close as they could get to what it might have looked like in 1808. They've done a great job. I think the most stunning feature is the elliptical spiral staircase that goes up all 3 floors. This little item put the "grand" in grand staircase. It would take 2 Scarletts to sweep down this baby. Put this on your Top 5 list of things to do.

OLD EXCHANGE BUILDING AND PROVOST DUNGEON

122 E Bay St, Charleston, 843-727-2165
www.oldexchange.org
HOURS: Open daily until 5 p.m.
ADMISSION: Minimal admission fee
Costumed guides lead tours of three floors of this historic building – formerly a Revolutionary prison & City Hall. The Declaration of Independence was read to the populace gathered below the balcony of this building. (In the ultimate irony, slaves were sold at auction very close to this building.) When it came time for South Carolina to ratify the Constitution, the vote was taken here. In the dungeon below, you'll see where Isaac Hayne was imprisoned before the British hanged him for supposedly breaking his parole during the war. As you can see by what I've told you here, this building has a unique history and the guides do a very entertaining job describing it to you.

OLD SLAVE MART MUSEUM
6 Chalmers St, Charleston, 843-958-6467
www.oldslavemartmuseum.com/
Exhibitions bring slavery to horrifying life in a way few museums do, addressing such topics as the stigma attached to the slave-trading profession and how slaves were dressed, shaved, fed and otherwise prepared for market day. In 1856, Charleston banned the buying and selling of slaves "outdoors." Some of the snobbier citizens thought this was a crude practice. But it was OK to sell slaves indoors in places like **Ryan's Mart**, where the first slave sold was a 20-year-old woman named Lucinda.

THE PITT STREET PHARMACY
111 Pitt St, Charleston (Mt. Pleasant), 843-884-4051
www.pittstreetpharmacy.com
This blast from the past dates back to 1938. Order a cherry Coke float from the old soda fountain.

POE'S TAVERN
2210 Middle St, Charleston, Sullivan's Island, 843-883-0083
www.poestavern.com
CUISINE: Burgers
DRINKS: Full Bar
SERVING: Lunch, Dinner & Late Night
PRICE RANGE: $$
Across the Sullivan's Island causeway you'll find this popular lunch spot in an old beach house. Try the spicy yellowfin tuna tacos with pineapple relish.

THE PRESERVATION SOCIETY OF CHARLESTON
147 King St, Charleston, 843-722-4630
www.preservationsociety.org/
ADMISSION: Nominal fee for tours of homes
NEIGHBORHOOD: Historic District
Founded in 1920, the oldest community-based historic preservation organization in the United States

continues its mission of protecting and advocating the Low Country's historic places. The Society offers a series of walking tours, lectures and symposiums.

RAVENEL BRIDGE
www.ravenelbridge.net
This graceful bridge was built because of the relentless pressure coming from a former state senator known in these parts as "Cousin" Arthur Ravenel. The $632 million bridge is supported by a pair of 572-foot-tall towers held together by 128 suspension cables. It was built withstand a 7.3 Richter scale earthquake (like the one that nearly leveled the city in 1886). The greenway is popular with strollers, cyclists, joggers and tourists Make sure you're one of them. A beautiful sight at night. There's a rooftop bar where you can see it at night to good effect. (See Nightlife chapter.)

SPOLETO FESTIVAL USA
14 George St, Charleston, 843-722-2764
www.spoletousa.org
Known as the city's artistic crown jewel, this world renowned festival offers 17 days and nights of incredible programming. The annual event fills Charleston's venues with opera, theater, dance, and a variety of music. Tickets sold for each event. Began in the mid 1970s.

ST JOHN'S LUTHERAN CHURCH
5 Clifford St, Charleston, 843-723-2426
www.stjohnscharleston.org
Boasting one of the oldest congregations of the Evangelical Lutheran Church in America, St. John's congregation dates back to the 1742 arrival of Dr. Henry Melchior Muhlenberg, the father of the Lutheran Church in America. Located in the Historic District, the present church edifice's Greek-Revival style was dedicated in 1818. Both the beautiful church and the cemetery are listed on the National Register of Historic Places. The church is steeped in history. The church's bell was given to the Confederacy for gunmetal. Now the tower rings with a 19-bell cast bronze carillon.

ST MICHAEL'S EPISCOPAL CHURCH
71 Broad St, Charleston, 843-723-0603
www.stmichaelschurch.net
The huge bronze bells ring every morning from this, the oldest church in Charleston. The surrounding streets are residential, and it's easy to imagine what life was like here 150 years ago. A walk along the waterfront will carry you past grand mansions to White Point Gardens (East Battery Street and Murray Boulevard). It was at this oak- and palmetto-lined sanctuary where townspeople watched the first shots fired on nearby Fort Sumter in 1861.

ST PHILIP'S EPISCOPAL CHURCH
142 Church St, Charleston, 843-722-7734
www.stphilipschurchsc.org
Located in the French Quarter area of Charleston, this National Historic Landmark was built in 1836. The brick church features a tower that was designed in the Wren-Gibbs tradition. The steeple was once used as a lighthouse to guide mariners into Charleston's harbor, one of only two steeples in the United States to have served that way. DuBose Heyward is buried here. (He wrote the book on which Gershwin's 1935 opera "Porgy & Bess" was based.) Seek out the grave of Sue Howard Hardy. Her ghost was supposedly captured on film in 1987.

TEAROOMS
If you find yourself in Charleston in the Spring, look for tearooms in the local churches. Even though they're called tearooms, they serve you lunch. The

"Post and Courier" lists them in the paper and also on their web site, www.postandcourier.com - you'll taste classic dishes like she-crab soup, okra soup, pimento cheese sandwiches, a Huguenot torte (with apples and pecans). You can buy homemade jams and preserves. Volunteers open these "tearooms" to raise money for the church.

U.S.S. YORKTOWN
PATRIOTS POINT NAVAL & MARITIME MUSEUM
40 Patriots Point Rd, Mt Pleasant, 843-884-2727
www.patriotspoint.org
USS Yorktown, one of 24 Essex-class aircraft carriers built during World War II for the United States Navy, and was the first ship of the Naval & Maritime Museum. The ship was named after the Battle of Yorktown during the American Revolutionary War. The museum consists of the USS Yorktown, USS Clamagore, the Medal of Honor Museum, 25 aircraft

from WWII to present and a Vietnam Support Base. Open daily. Admission fee.

WALKING TOUR WITH MARTINE DULLES
www.charlestonpromenades.com
PRICES & LENGTH OF TOUR VARY
Professional tour guide **Martine Dulles** used to be a docent at the Metropolitan in New York. But here she's known for her knowledgeable walking tours of Charleston, with lots to say about the city's art, architecture and history. Tour places such as Old City Market, The Powder Magazine, St. Michael's Episcopal Church, Rainbow Row, The Citadel, and beautiful Charleston homes.

WHITE POINT GARDENS
2 Murray Blvd., Charleston, 843-724-7327
www.charlestonparksconservancy.org
Located in the heart of Charleston's historic district, White Point Gardens is a 5.7-acre public park and prominent landmark offering a spectacular view of Fort Sumter and Charleston Harbor. First used as a public garden in 1837, it became a fortification of the city during the Civil War. Visitors can view the impressive display of historic mortars and cannons from the Civil War. The park also has a variety of historical markers, statues and monuments.

Chapter 7
SHOPPING & SERVICES

For many years, King Street was the main shopping street in Charleston, but chain stores now proliferate, taking the charm and uniqueness away. Move on to upper King Street, north of Marion Square, where you'll discover one-of-a-kind shops and high-end concept restaurants. Snatch the one-page guide to parking and neighborhood restaurants distributed everywhere.

BEN SILVER COLLECTION
149 King St, Charleston, 843-577-4556
www.bensilver.com
A shop for gentlemen who enjoy quality and excellence in their fashions. Here you'll find classically styled jackets, suits, shirts, ties, socks and shoes. They also feature a nice selection of evening attire and fine jewelry for men. If you're in town over Christmas, stop in to buy (or just to look at) their silk ties designed with holiday trees. The cuff links are gorgeous.

BLUE BICYCLE BOOKS
420 King St, Charleston, 843-722-2666
www.bluebicyclebooks.com
Founded in 1995 as Boomer's Books, the store became Blue Bicycle Books in 2007 when purchased by local writer Jonathan Sanchez. The store, known as a used, rare and local bookstore, features 50,000 volumes of the most complete collection of used books covering subjects like Civil War, military history, literary fiction and hardback classics.

CHARLESTON FARMERS MARKET
Marion Square: 329 Meeting St, Charleston, 843-724-7305
www.charlestonfarmersmarket.com
A bustling downtown market where you can buy pickled watermelon rind, sweetgrass baskets and flower arrangements that make use of old windows.

Be prepared to fight your way through the throngs buying their week's supply of groceries or lining up for fresh crepes. $4.50 and up.

CITY LIGHTS COFFEE HOUSE
141 Market St, Charleston, 843-853-7067
No Website
It's an intimate spot to unwind with a glass of wine or delicious carrot cake.

CROGHAN'S JEWEL BOX
308 King St, Charleston, 843-723-3594
www.croghansjewelbox.com
This is a family owned business that's been here for about 100 years. You have to ring a little bell to get into the place, but once you do, you'll be captivated by their impressive collection of estate jewelry, including Tahitian and South Sea pearls, antique brooches and lockets. They have some odd-looking bow ties made from S.C. turkey feathers.

FINICKY FILLY
303 King St, Charleston, 843-534-0203
www.thefinickyfilly.com
Located in the heart of downtown Charleston, this women's wear shop offers a variety of fashions for all ages. Names like Tory Burch and Lela Rose, and interesting jewelry as well. You'll find fashions for mothers and daughters ranging from moderate to high-end fashions. (It's owned by a mother and daughter, so that makes sense.)

GEORGE C. BIRLANT & CO
191 King St, Charleston, 843-722-3842
www.birlant.com
This is among the largest of the area's antiques dealers.

HARRIS TEETER
www.harristeeter.com
Customer Service: 800 432 6111
This is a grocery chain based in North Carolina with several locations in the Charleston area. Visit store locator on the website.

KAMINSKY'S MOST EXCELLENT CAFÉ
78 N Market St, Charleston, 843-853-8270
www.kaminskys.com
A boisterous spot for sweets like Toll House cookie pie ($3.95 a slice).

LILY
196 King St, Charleston, 843-577-7633
www.lilycharleston.com

A beautiful shop filled with gorgeous, artfully curated pieces for the fashionable lady. Items featured include vintage jewelry, scarves, stationary, handbags, and exquisite gift items.

M. DUMAS & SONS
294 King St, Charleston, 843-723-8603
www.mdumasandsons.com
Open since 1917, this shop features fine clothing for men and women. Shop here for custom fitted suits, preppy clothes done Southern-style and that perfect outfit for the Kentucky Derby. Madras sports coats, needlepoint belts, boxer shorts with pennants. You get the idea.

MACAROON BOUTIQUE
45 John St, Charleston, 843-577-5441
www.macaroonboutique.com
This tiny shop offers a variety of specialties including scones, croissants, and macaroons, all made by the owner. There are several varieties and flavors of each but the macaroons are the best.

MAGAR HATWORKS
57 Cannon St, Charleston, 843-345-4483
www.magarhatworks.com
Call for appointment, a millinery where Leigh Magar makes recherché hats ($175 to $700) that sell at high-end stores like Barneys New York.

MARION SQUARE FARMERS' MARKET
329 Meeting St, Charleston, 843-724-7305
www.charlestonfarmersmarket.com

Saturday-only, from April - December
A favorite market for both locals and visitors, this Saturday-only farmers' market features hundreds of local vendors selling fresh meats and poultry right from the farm. You'll also find a variety of handmade foods including sausages, meats, pates, and jams. Lots of entertainment and places to stop for lunch. Great place to gets gifts for friends back home. Try the wild boar black-truffle cheese from **Charleston Artisan Cheesehouse** or some stone ground grits, the very best. Go to **Mike's** for a bag of moist juicy boiled peanuts or to **Barbara's** for a sweetgrass basket. Or **Roti Rolls** mac n cheese sandwiches.

MARKET HALL
www.thecharlestoncitymarket.com/
This Greek revival temple built in 1841 now is home to a thrilling open-air mall at the intersection of

Meeting and Market Streets. The northern end has a number of small, enclosed shops that sell hats, jewelry and Christmas ornaments, while the southern end is filled with jewelers, antiques dealers, painters, potters and weavers who make sweetgrass baskets — an African-American art form that was named the state's official handicraft. Noteworthy vendors include **Turtle Creek** (843-884-7521; www.puzzleboxguy.com), which sells hand-carved puzzle boxes made of cedar, walnut and canarywood (from about $20), and **Else Olsen**, who sells handmade jade and tiger eye necklaces ($25 to $45).

PARHAM & CO
1849 Ave F, North Charleston, 843-722-5344
www.parhamandcompany.com
Established in 1933, this place offers a great selection of European antique furniture and decorative pieces for the house. The perfect place to find beautiful one-of-a-kind traditional antiques, Everything from polo balls to tea caddies and jewelry.

READ BROTHERS STEREO AND FABRIC STORE
593 King St, Charleston, 843-723-7276
www.readbrothers.com
Established in 1912, you'll get the feeling that some of the bizarre items for sale in here were in stock when the store opened a century ago. Wonderful browsing.

SILVER VAULT OF CHARLESTON
195 King St, Charleston, 843-722-0631
www.silvervaultcharleston.com
This place is a Charleston tradition. Here you'll find an incredible selection of superior decorative arts with a strong emphasis on silver and brass. Owner Charlotte Crabtree has silver from France, England and of course the U.S.

WILDFLOUR PASTRY
73 Spring St, Charleston, 843-327-2621

www.wildflourpastrycharleston.com
Created an instant tradition with "sticky bun Sundays." A steady stream of cravers comes through the door in search of a warm, chewy, generously pecaned confection ($2.70). Those with less of a sweet tooth will be happy with crumbly fruity or savory scones ($2 and up) or a hardboiled Sea Island egg (60 cents).

WORTHWHILE
268 King St, Charleston, 843-723-4418
www.shopworthwhile.com
Located in the historic **McIntosh Seed House**, this place offers collections of beautiful objects from around the globe. You'll find an ever-changing selection of textural women's and children's clothing and shoes. Brands offered include: Christian Peau, Marsell and Uma Wang. Browse through the shelves of unique products, whimsical housewares, bedding, fragrances and bath products, Moroccan slippers by Proud Mary.

INDEX

:

: Mexican, 54

1

167 RAW, 21

A

African-American Focus Tour, 95
American, 32, 35, 39, 50, 66
American (New), 50
American (New),, 65
American (New)/, 60
American (Traditional)/, 54

B

Barbecue, 40
BASICO AT MIXSON BATH & RACQUET CLUB, 82
BATTERY CARRIAGE HOUSE INN, 9
BATTERY, THE, 82
BELMOND CHARLESTON PLACE HOTEL, 9
BEN SILVER COLLECTION, 107
BERTHA'S, 22
BICYCLE SHOPPE, 82
BIN 152, 77
BIRLANT GEORGE C & CO, 109
BLACK TAP, 65
blacksmith and cooper workshops, 95
BLUE BICYCLE BOOKS, 107

BOONE HALL PLANTATION, 83
BOWENS ISLAND RESTAURANT, 23
Breakfast, 25
BROAD STREET, 8
BULLDOG TOURS, 83
Burgers, 63, 65
BUTCHER & BEE, 24

C

CAFÉ ROUX, 72
CANNON GREEN, 24
CAVIAR AND BANANAS, 25
CHARLESTON BLACK CAB COMPANY, 7
CHARLESTON CITY MARKET, 84
CHARLESTON CULINARY TOURS, 84
CHARLESTON FARMERS MARKET, 107
CHARLESTON GRILL, 26
CHARLESTON HARBOR RESORT & MARINA, 10
CHARLESTON KAYAK, 85
CHARLESTON STAGE COMPANY, 85
Charleston Stage Theatre Company, 86
CHARLESTON STROLLS, 85
CHEZ NOUS, 27
CHICK & PATTY'S, 72
CHUBBY FISH, 27
CIRCA 1886, 28
Circa 1996, 17
CITY LIGHTS COFFEE HOUSE, 108
CLOSED FOR BUSINESS, 78
COAST, 29

COASTAL EXPEDITIONS, 86
COCKTAIL CLUB, 78
CODFATHER, 30
Coffee & Tea, 65
CONGREGATION KAHAL KADOSH BETH ELOHIM, 86
CROGHAN'S JEWEL BOX, 108

D

DARLING OYSTER BAR, 30
DAVE's CARRY-OUT, 31
Desserts, 54
DEWBERRY, 10
DOCK STREET THEATRE, 86
DRAYTON HALL, 87

E

EARLY BIRD DINER, 32
EDMONDSTON-ALSTON HOUSE, 87
EDMUND'S OAST, 32
EVO PIZZERIA & CRAFT BAKERY, 33

F

FIG, 34
FINICKY FILLY, 109
FIREFLY DISTILLERY, 88
FOLLY BEACH CRAB SHACK, 35
FORT SUMTER TOURS, 88
Francis Marion Hotel, 67
FRANCIS MARION HOTEL, 11
FREE REIGN, 72
FRENCH QUARTER INN, 11

G

GALLERY CHUMA, 89
Gastropub, 32
GATEWAY WALK, 90
GAULART & MALICLET, 35
GEORGE C. BIRLANT & CO, 109
GIBBES MUSEUM OF ART, 91
GIN JOINT, 78
GLASS ONION, 36
GOAT SHEEP COW, 37
GRAY LINE TOURS, 91
GRIFFON, 79
GRILL 225, 37
Grille225, 15
GROCERY, 39
GULLAH GRUB, 40
GULLAH TOURS, 91

H

HALL'S CHOPHOUSE, 41
HALSEY INSTITUTE OF CONEMPORARY ART, 92
HAMPTON INN-HISTORIC DISTRICT, 12
HANK'S SEAFOOD RESTAURANT, 41
HANNIBAL'S KITCHEN, 42
HARRIS TEETER, 109
HENRIETTA'S, 42
Henrietta's Brasserie, 11
HIGH COTTON, 43
HOLIDAY INN HOTEL CHARLESTON HISTORIC DISTRICT, 12
HUNLEY, 93

HUSK, 44

I

Italian, 70

J

Japanese, 74
JESTINE'S KITCHEN, 45
JOHN RUTLEDGE HOUSE INN, 13

K

KAMINSKY'S MOST EXCELLENT CAFÉ, 46, 109
Kayaking Tours, 95
KINGS COURTYARD INN, 14

L

Lata, Mike, 34
LE FARFALLE, 46
LEON'S FINE POULTRY & OYSTERS, 47
LEON'S OYSTER SHOP, 47
LEWIS BARBECUE, 48
LILY, 109
LITTLE JACK'S TAVERN, 49
LITTLE MISS HA, 72
LOST DOG CAFÉ, 50

M

M. DUMAS & SONS, 110
MACAROON BOUTIQUE, 110
Macintosh, 78

MACINTOSH, 50
MAGAR HATWORKS, 110
MAGNOLIA CEMETERY, 93
MAGNOLIA PLANTATION & GARDENS, 94
MAGNOLIAS, 51
MARION SQUARE FARMERS' MARKET, 110
MARKET PAVILION HOTEL, 14
MCCRADY'S, 53
Mediterranean, 24, 57
MERCANTILE AND MASH, 54
MERROWS GARDEN BAR, 72
Mexican, 68
MIDDLETON PLACE, 15
MIDDLETON PLACE PLANTATION, 95
MILLS HOUSE, 15
MINERO, 54
MOUNT PLEASANT PRESBYTERIAN CHURCH, 96
MUSE RESTAURANT AND WINE BAR, 55
MYNT, 79

N

NANA'S SEAFOOD & SOUL, 56
NATHANIEL RUSSELL HOUSE, 96
NOTSO-HOSTEL, 15

O

OBSTINATE DAUGHTER, 57
OLD EXCHANGE BUILDING AND PROVOST DUNGEON, 97
OLD SLAVE MART MUSEUM, 98
ORDINARY, 58

P

PARHAM & CO, 112
PARK CAFÉ, 59
PAVILION BAR, 79
PEARLZ OYSTER BAR, 59
PENINSULA GRILL, 60
PITT STREET PHARMACY, 98
Pizza, 57
Planter's Inn, 60
PLANTERS INN, 16
POE'S TAVERN, 99
POOGAN'S PORCH RESTAURANT, 61
PRESERVATION SOCIETY, 99
PURLIEU, 62

R

RAVENEL BRIDGE, 100
READ BROTHER STEREO AND FABRIC STORE, 113
REBEL TAQUERIA, 72
RENZO, 62
RITA'S SEASIDE GRILLE, 63
RODNEY SCOTT'S BBQ, 63
ROOFTOP, 64
RUTLEDGE CAB CO, 65
Ryan's Mart, 98

S

Sandwiches, 24, 25
Seafood, 23, 35, 40, 41, 47, 57, 59, 63

SHELLMORE, THE, 65
SILVER VAULT OF CHARLESTON, 113
Slave Experience Tour, 95
Soul Food, 56
Southern, 36, 45, 47, 67, 70
Spoleto, 86
SPOLETO FESTIVAL, 100
ST JOHN'S LUTHERAN CHURCH, 101
ST MICHAEL'S EPISCOPAL CHURCH, 102
ST PHILIP'S EPISCOPAL CHURCH, 103
STARS ROOFTOP & GRILL ROOM, 66
Steakhouse, 60, 66
SUSHI WA IZAKAYA, 72
SWAMP FOX, 67

T

TACO BOY, 68
Taiwanese, 74
TATTOOED MOOSE, 69
TEAROOMS, 103
TOURS, 8
TWO MEETING STREET INN, 16

U

U.S.S. YORKTOWN, 104

V

Vendue Hotel, 64
Vietnamese, 74
VIRGINIA'S ON KING, 70
VOODOO TIKI BAR, 80

W

WALKING TOUR WITH MARTINE DULLES, 105
WENTWORTH MANSION, 17
WHITE POINT GARDENS, 105
WILD OLIVE RESTAURANT, 70
WILDFLOUR PASTRY, 113
WORKMEN'S CAFÉ, 71
WORKSHOP, 71
WORTHWHILE, 114
WRECK OF THE RICHARD & CHARLENE, 73

X

XIAO BAO BISCUIT, 74

Z

ZERO GEORGE, 18
Zero George Street Hotel, 75
ZERO RESTAURANT + BAR, 74

Other Books by the Same Author

Andrew Delaplaine has written in widely varied fields: screenplays, novels (adult and juvenile), travel writing, journalism. His books are available in quality bookstores, libraries, as well as all online retailers.

JACK HOUSTON ST. CLAIR POLITICAL THRILLERS

On Election night, as China and Russia mass soldiers on their common border in preparation for war, there's a tie in the Electoral College that forces the decision for President into the House of Representatives as mandated by the Constitution. The incumbent Republican President, working through his Aide for Congressional Liaison, uses the Keystone File, which contains dirt on every member of Congress, to blackmail members into supporting the Republican candidate. The action runs from Election Night in November to Inauguration Day on

January 20. Jack Houston St. Clair runs a small detective agency in Miami. His father is Florida Governor Sam Houston St. Clair, the Republican candidate. While he tries to help his dad win the election, Jack also gets hired to follow up on some suspicious wire transfers involving drug smugglers, leading him to a sunken narco-sub off Key West that has $65 million in cash in its hull.

AFTER THE OATH: DAY ONE
AFTER THE OATH: MARCH WINDS
WEDDING AT THE WHITE HOUSE

Only three months have passed since Sam Houston St. Clair was sworn in as the new President, but a lot has happened.
Returning from Vienna where he met with Russian and Chinese diplomats, Sam is making his way back to Flagler Hall in Miami, his first trip home since being inaugurated. Son Jack is in the midst of turmoil of his own back in Miami, dealing with various dramas, not the least of which is his increasing alienation from Babylon Fuentes and his growing attraction to the seductive Lupe Rodriguez. Fernando Pozo addresses new problems as he struggles to expand Cuba's secret operations in the U.S., made even more difficult as U.S.-Cuban relations thaw. As his father returns home, Jack knows Sam will find as much trouble at home as he did in Vienna.

www.ingramcontent.com/pod-product-compliance
Lightning Source LLC
Chambersburg PA
CBHW061448040426
42450CB00007B/1268